the Idler

ISSUE 34 | WINTER 2004

First published in Great Britain in 2004 by
Idle Limited
Studio 20, 24 - 28a Hatton Wall
London EC1N 8JH
Tel: 020 7691 0320
Fax: 020 7691 0321
e-mail: theidlers@idler.co.uk

ISBN 0-9 536720-9-3

Editor: Tom Hodgkinson   Creative Director: Gavin Pretor-Pinney
Deputy Editor: Dan Kieran
Editor-at Large: Matthew De Abaitua
Designer: Sonia Ortiz Alcón
Managing Editor: Edward Sage
Advertising and Promotional Director: Will Hogan
Literary Editor: Tony White
Music Editor: Will Hodgkinson
Sports Editor: John Moore
Contributing Editors: Greg Rowland, Ian Vince
Editorial Assistant: Christianna Currie
Cover: James Jarvis
Advertising: Jamie Dwelly at Cabbell 020 8971 8450

What is **the Idler**?

The Idler is a magazine that celebrates
freedom, fun and the fine art
of doing nothing.

We believe that idleness is unjustly
criticized in modern society when it is,
in fact, a vital component of a happy life.

We want to comfort and inspire you with
uplifting philosophy, satire and
reflection, as well as giving
practical information to help in the quest
for the idle life.

NOBODY EVER SAID YOU ARE WHAT YOU DRINK. BUT JUST IN CASE.

If the taste inspectors were to burst into your lounge unexpectedly, what would they find on your table? Something suggesting an undiscerning temperament? Or a more complimentary character witness, like Fuller's legendary ESB? More awards from around the world have been showered on ESB than any other beer in its class, in recognition of its full, uniquely rich and deliciously fruity flavour. Which means you and your fellow connoisseurs will be confident your coffee table will pass with flying colours.

IDLER CONTRIBUTORS

Who are the idlers?

Jad Adams is a writer and TV producer specialising in the decadence of the 1890s. His books include: *Madder Music StrongerWine: the Life of Ernest Dowson* (2000) and *Hideous Absinthe: a History of the Devil in a Bottle* (2004)

Eddie Argos is the lead singer of Art Brut

Marc Baines runs the Salty Cellar club in Glasgow

Joan Bakewell currently presents *Belief* for BBC Radio 3. Her autobiography, *The Centre of the Bed*, was published in the autumn of 2003

Simon Browne runs the Number 11 The Quay restaurant in Ilfracombe

Sean Butler is a Canadian journalist

Nemone Caldwell is not available to take your call. Please leave your name and number and she'll get back to you: nemone@hedled.com

Edward Cumming is 17 and a pupil at Westminster School

Matthew De Abaitua is always available

Brian Dean runs the excellent website anxietyculture.com

Chris Draper is an illustrator and beekeeper who regularly contributes to *New Scientist* and the *Independent*

Bill Drummond is a serial father

Hannah Dyson draws anthropomorphic creatures and other beings

Liz Emerson takes really nice photos with her camera and with her mind. She will gladly make pictures of you and your family or your buildings on polite request

David Hallows is an illustrator discovering the beauty of old Stax recordings

Paul Hamilton has had an American battleship named after him

Jeff Harrison is a painter, illustrator and misanthropist from east London

Joe Harrison is a comical, talented

all-round good guy, need we say more?

Anthony Haythornthwaite is an illustrator for hire, to contact him email aqh@lineone.net

Will Hodgkinson is a journalist based in London

Will Hogan is a raconteur, scribe and used ad salesman. He's available at will@idler.co.uk

Leo Hollis lives in London and is a writer and editor. He makes a mean spaghetti Bolognese

Sandra Howgate has been busy illustrating for various publications, and not had enough time for idle pleasures

Tony Husband is an award winning cartoonist who works for the *Times*, the *Express*, the *Sun*, *Private Eye* and many many more. He also performs a live cartoon poetry interactive stage show with Ian Macmillan. For more information visit tonyhusband.co.uk

Sarah Janes is a multi-tasking rock'n'rolling journalist, ex-shoplifter and writer who lives in Brighton

James Jarvis is a master of illustration

Jerome K Jerome's *The Idle Thoughts of an Idle Fellow* has just been re-published by Snow Books

Fanny Johnstone writes about sex and cars in the *Daily Telegraph*

Andrew Kendall is a rock'n'roll photographer and multi-media man

Dan Kieran is the *Idler*'s Deputy Editor and editor of the recently published *Crap Towns 2* and *Crap Jobs*

Chloe King is an illustrator. She can be found at rideem@boozers.moonfruit.com

Rowley Leigh is head chef at Kensington Place, food writer for the *FT* and author of *No Place Like Home*

Tanya Ling avoids housework at all costs

Sophie Lodge is an illustrator and

travelling around Ireland cooking soup for people.

We report back from the US initiative Take Back Your Time Day, one of the many ideas currently challenging the supremacy of work. And the one and only Joan Bakewell writes stirring words on her own rejection of conventional career values. The matchless Rowley Leigh introduces our new Idle Cook section with recipes for those with time on their hands, and in the back section we give some advice on birds, bees,, tea and looking after yourself. In our new travel section we go to Mexico and Fiji, and find attitudes to work a good deal more relaxed than our own. In

music, we welcome Art Brut with their own guide to becoming a pop star, plus we profile medievalists Circulus and look at the intense career of Peter Doherty.

And for all readers who have not yet come across his work, we print some extracts from the brilliant Giro Playboy.

We really feel that the ideas we are exploring are gaining ground and welcome everyone to join our gentle, joyful, easy revolution.

Thank you very much and now we are going into hibernation and shall see you again in the spring.

TOM HODGKINSON
Tom@idler.co.uk

EDITOR'S LETTER

FOOD IS MEANT to be a pleasure and it is meant to be nourishing. But across the West, it has been debased into something which at best merely refuels us on our way to work and which at worst actually makes us ill, physically, mentally and spiritually. Modern food leaves us wanting more. This is the inevitable result of the processes of industrialisation which began in around 1750 and which are still moving us along today. In our Food issue, we talk to Joanna Blythman, author of *Shopped*, about the horror of modern supermarkets. Penny Rimbaud argues that the decline in food quality is directly related to the rise of capitalism, while our feature on Slow Food suggests that there may be some pleasurable modes of resistance available. Bill Drummond writes on his latest project, the Soup Line, which involves uncle Bill

TANYA LING

SLOWING DOWN P90

More Contents THE IDLER, ISSUE 34, WINTER 2004

BARTENDER,
THERE'S *CUCUMBER* IN MY GIN.

Fear not, all the surprises of this gin taste marvelous. **HENDRICK'S®** *is instilled with juniper, coriander, citrus peel and a particularly luscious infusion of rose petal and* **cucumber.**

Hendrick's Gin is avaialable at Harvey Nichols, Peckhams (Scotland), Gerry's of Old Compton Street, drinkon.com, Lea & Sandemann, thewhiskyexchange.com and other unusual retailers.

⌘ HENDRICK'S ⌘
A MOST UNUSUAL GIN

HENDRICKSGIN.COM

SUPERMARKET SLAVES P66

Contents THE IDLER, ISSUE 34, WINTER 2004

international gypsy

Pete Loveday is a jobbing artist, self-buried in Devon. He created the legendary Russell comics. Find out more at ccnewz.com

Keith Mahoney is with the band

Edwin Marney is an illustrator who generally works for dull business magazines. Visit his website at edwinmarney.co.uk

Jenny O'Mahony has never had a real job and would like to keep it that way

Sonia Ortiz Alcón helped lay out this mag and her work can be seen at foreignoffice.com

James Parker is a young Dad and writer living far, far away in Boston, Mass

Kevin Parr is a writer and angler. He can sometimes be found on the A33 near Winchester

Alan Porter is director of the Chocolate Society

Orlando Radice is a latin lover and freelance writer based in Bologna

Penny Rimbaud, like most of the great philosophers before him, is a committed writer, and, like all of them, without exception, he is a confirmed wanker: alone in an absurd universe, to whom else is the *überidler* able to turn?

John Riordan thinks Western culture peaked with Motown. He really, really wants a cat

Greg Rowland is a legitimate businessman

Edward Sage is the *Idler*'s Managing Editor

Jock Scot is a poet searching for a patron

Dr. Sleeves' bespoke CD compilation Mad as a *Badger's Armpit: a Partial Gazeteer to the Pastoral Sounds of Old Albion* will be released by Post in December

Philip Smiley illustrated The Truth

Michael Smith is The Giro Playboy

Gwyn Vaughn Roberts lives in Wales and can only produce work when his mental state is a fine balance of energy and misery

Ian Vince is a left-handed, Mac-compatible, asthmatic comedy writer, clearly looking for some kind of niche market. He runs socialscrutiny.org

JOCK SCOT

JENNY O'MAHONY

JOAN BAKEWELL

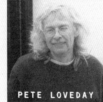

PETE LOVEDAY

GREG ROWLAND

JANES

FANNY JOHNSTONE

Chris Watson invites you to sample some king-size art and design at chris-watson.co.uk

Tony White is the *Idler*'s Literary Editor

Chris Yates is a legendary fisherman, photographer, master of idleness and author of *The Secret Carp* (Merlin Unwin)

NOTES FROM THE COUCH

JEFF HARRISON

THE IDLER'S DIARY

MEGAPHONE, BEER, BANNERS

YOUR editor jumped up on a lamp post on Clerkenwell Green in September, and harangued a crowd with his megaphone to launch his book, *How To Be Idle*. Barrels of Fuller's London Pride and large quantities of Hendrick's Gin were handed out to fellow anti-work protestors.

The rally had been preceeded by a demonstration on Waterloo Bridge where harried commuters were presented with an idler's manifesto. Truly, the revolution is here! Anarchy! Freedom! Love! YOUR creative director would like to alert you to his new project, the Cloud Appreciation Society, aimed at furthering the enjoyment and understanding of clouds around the world. The Society's website will be launching shortly, where you will be able to read of the derivation of "cloud nine", discover how many elephants a typical cloud weighs and hear of adventures to Australia to see a cloud that glider pilots surf. The site will be an invaluable resource for cloud gazers young and old and its visitors will be invited to upload their own cloud pictures as well as to become members of this soon-to-be-esteemed society. www.cloudappreciationsociety.org.

TO THE Simon Finch art gallery in Portobello Road for the launch of Michael Smith's brilliant *Giro Playboy* boxed set. Michael gave a great performance in the downstairs gallery. The event was almost spoiled by an unfortunate drain smell which wafted up from the floor, but luckily the smoking restrictions were relaxed which allowed Mr Jock Scot to light his pipe and fill the room with the sweet aroma of pipe tobacco to mask the stink. Afterwards we repaired to the pub over the road where everyone fell over. See page 38 for some selections.

OCTOBER saw the release of two more Idler books, *Crap Towns II* and *Crap Jobs*. Both are written, once again, by our readers and both are witty attacks on two failed modern institutions: towns and jobs. We're going to keep running your best entries in the magazine and if you have any good stories send them to us at dan@idler.co.uk THE IDLER'S book releases were marred by a nasty rip-off courtesy of none other than the BBC. Their publication *Crap Cars* looks rather like our books, feels rather like our books and the average reader could be forgiven for thinking that it is one of our books. Let us tell you straight that *Crap Cars* is an inferior product and nothing to do with the Idler. The BBC really ought to know better. We did consider suing but decided instead that we couldn't be bothered and will instead content ourselves with talking about the matter loudly in the pub and not watching BBC3.

WE SALUTE the Trades Unions Congress for their new campaign to introduce three more bank holidays a year. Britain enjoys only eight bank holidays compared to the average of eleven indulged by our less work-obsessed neighbours in Europe. They ran a poll which asked 20,000 people how they would spend the proposed October bank holiday. Nearly 60% said "lie in and rest at home" or "take a weekend break away" compared with only 1% opting to "take work home with you" and a delightfully small 3% who would spend the time shopping. Clearly we are a nation of idlers. And the TUC is turning out to be quite idler-friendly, perhaps surprisingly for a union. Another of their campaigns centres on the billions of pounds worth of unpaid overtime that the

CRAP BOOK

Britsh worker contributes annually to the cause of capital. They also share an enemy with us idlers, which is the CBI, a spokesperson from whom is always appearing on the *Today* programme bleating about "hours lost to British Industry" by the skiving British worker. The CBI's reaction to the TUC's bank holiday campaign was predictably joyless, prim and self-sacrificing, while also making the old and discredited link between long hours and greater productivity. "If we allow ourselves more free time we would all end up paying because lower productivity can mean less investment, fewer jobs and higher prices. We suspect people who would be most delighted would be in competitor countries such as China, India, France and Germany." Cunts. It's time to rise up, comrades!

READERS' LETTERS

Write to us at: **The Idler**, Studio 20, 24-28A Hatton Wall, London EC1N 8JH or tom@idler.co.uk

EVERY LETTER WINS A T-SHIRT!

Dear Idlers,
I must say keep up the great effort of not quite total lackadaisicalness that is your unique publication. I had felt slightly inclined to berate you for not producing it quite frequently enough, but on not inconsiderable reflection you have just about the perfect schedule as I still haven't quite finished reading the last two issues – despite them having been floating around my mostly unthumbed bookshelf for what seems like a few years. I had opportunity to read a few of your articles more completely on a recent Nice – London commute (it is not only infinitely more pleasant but in fact also cheaper to loaf on the Cote d'Azur and commute to London for the odd bit of work than most people may imagine).

Until reading these articles I had never considered myself an idler or flâneur, but now I see that ever since I took the step of reducing my working week to four days so that I could spend more time sprawled on my sofa sipping Armagnac and listening to kitsch lounge music, that I have in fact been working towards the true goal of every idler – doing no work whatsoever. I am now very near that goal with another 40-odd years to enjoy before I retire, although as a presently part-time idler am committed to two days per week of graft as this helps keep my fridge stocked with the smoked Islay venison for which I have a penchant... To all would-be idlers I say invest more of your time in leisure and life will taste so much truer; lead those who toil solely for their masters pleasure to seek the self-fulfilment of the idler!
Jacob
Have you succeeded in becoming an idler? Send us your stories to: tom@idler.co.uk

Dear Idlers,
Howdy there, as we say in some parts of America. Hopefully, we'll be saying it less after the November election. In any case, I discovered the Idler on a recent trip to the UK, and agree completely that laziness has been given an undeserved bum rap.
Wally Bear
Is it true that US workers get only two weeks holiday a year? Stateside idlers, we want to hear from you.

Dear Idlers,
I've been an Idler all my life (almost 43 years now), although have introduced myself to people as a "slacker", which is the nearest term I'd heard for people like myself. Idler will do fine, though. Since graduating (in philosophy, of course) all those years ago, I failed to develop a healthy respect for "work", in spite of enjoying about eight years of employment in a sales office. Bringing up my two sons gave me an excuse for being at home, which was just about acceptable to others, but I never went back... It's not work that I object to, it's the selling of so much time, the commitment – and a poxy two weeks off a year for good behaviour.
I look around and see madness: I mean, working mothers... don't even go there! They bust a gut all week, only to hand over the money they earn to the child-minder? Two hours commuting a day? Like I said, madness.
Didn't mean to go on, just wanted to touch base with a fellow Idler spirits. Thanks for introducing me to the guilt-free concept (I was just about there already), and to say I look forward to enjoying your site.
Lorraine Turner

Dear Idlers,

I have looked at your website for the first time whilst listening to Tom on Radio 4's Sloth special. Most interesting.

However, I am not sure whether you have given thought to the concept of various levels of status or qualification in Idling. What do I mean? Simple: do you idle professionally or are you a gentleman idler? Is there not a place for categories – even awards? Imagine: Apprentice Idler; Novitiate; and perhaps the Order of the Idler, granted each year to nominated figures, nationally and internationally. Patron? Eric Idle...?

Thank you
Roger Carter
Thank you, Roger, but we're not sure that we really want to introduce a competitive element into the world of idling. Shouldn't just declaring that you are an idler be enough? The palm, the oak and bays are distractions.

Dear Idlers,

Yes, I must say what a great site. It has actually lifted the doom and gloom I'm in now. But I would advise more content based on family, relationships, the future, etc etc...
Ed
The future is a big subject but we'll give it a go.

Dear Idlers,

I have managed to perfect the art whilst still being employed (undiscovered), but am about to take it up full time (discovered), due to force of circumstances you might say. Sadly, my kind of idling costs! Any advice on how an idle Idler might fund the easy life?
Jeremy Jones
This is the eternal question and in the capitalist economy there are no easy answers. We would suggest cutting down your expenses and starting your own small cottage industry. Some of us have greatly enjoyed growing vegetables. Stealing what you need is another option. Good luck!

A WINTER WARMER

Benylin is rightly thought of as a winter drink, a vintage "discussed" – to use the Byronic term for imbibing – in much the same way that a bottle of good quality port is thought of as bringing relief from the omnipresent depression of the British winter: Apothecary: "A family bottle of Benylin and a crate of lemonade, sir?" "Yes, apothecary, taking to my bed for the winter. Can't be laid short of a 'Shrewsbury Classic' or two." "Very good sir."

The Ludlow Lady (Serves 4)
1 bottle of chilled quality champagne
1 bottle of Benylin expectorant (drowsy)
Method Pour the bottle of Benylin into four champagne flutes in equal measure. Top up with the chilled champagne. Following Ludlow's recent inclusion on the Northern tube line (Morden to Edinburgh), it has become fashionable to add a pinch of cocaine, making this the speedball of Benylin cocktails. It is then sometimes referred to as a "Clapham Carriage". Feisty.

DR SLEEVES

SKIVERS

HEROES AND VILLAINS...

Larry David

His largely improvised TV show 'Curb Your Enthusiasm' just keeps getting better. Railing against the banal stupidities of modern life, it's like Hancock in Beverly Hills. Here's Larry in Starbucks: "I'll have a vanilla... one of those vanilla bullshit things. You know, whatever you want, some vanilla bullshit latte cappa thing. Whatever you got."

The Yes Men

Top new satirical dooumentary in which Andy and Mike pose as spokespeople for the World Trade Organisation, travelling to corporate conferences the world over. Posing as a WTO expert on CNBC, Andy insists "a market in human rights violations can allow countries that want to abuse people to buy 'Justice Vouchers' from those who don't." Priceless. See www.theyesmen.org.

Camping

Hotels are stultifying and hushed and a shared holiday in a villa in Tuscany invariably ends up in one of the other guest's wanky novels. No, it is camping for us. The egalitarianism of nature! A bottle of scotch under the stars! A blustery walk along the Devon-Cornwall coastal path! And fisherman's hat we are truly throwing off the shackles of cool.

Timothy the Tortoise

Rory-Knight Bruce's lovely biography is out now. Timothy died this April and was over 160 years old.

LARRY DAVID AND FRIENDS AND, ABOVE, TIMOTHY THE TORTOISE

STRIVERS

...OF THE IDLE UNIVERSE

TV Advertising

Perhaps we are becoming more sensitive in our old age yet it seems to us that in this multi-channel multimedia world adverts are becoming more aggressive than ever. Once a parochial profession, advertising has become a grotesque circus, a pseudo-art propped up pseudo-science and practised by pseudo-intellectuals. Brainwashing? Braindirtying.

Sky Customer magazine

According to the masthead, it takes sixty-two people to flop this piece of shit onto our doormats every month. It wouldn't be so bad if every one of its 114 pages (that's not even two pages per staff member, P45 fans) wasn't filled with marketing department approved guff and "I-can't-bear-to-look-at-what-I'm-typing" film reviews. Even the one-star movies are described as "watchable".

Crap BBC

Dear Mr Michael Grade, exactly which aspect of your public service remit suggests your corporation should rip off the one commercially viable project a bunch of struggling alternative journos have managed in a decade? *Crap Towns/Jobs* are the only thing keeping us in opium and whores, how dare the BBC do a *Crap Cars* book! Is this what the license fee buys us? Plagiarism?

Nigella Lawson

She recently argued that meaningless toil is preferable to inactivity, that she'd rather clock on than do nothing. This is the crazy thinking from a powerhouse who has done so much to make other women feel inadequate, and to whom inserting the word "rather" every three paragraphs makes for good writing. I suppose it's the old Jewish work ethic. Daughter of a politician. Ambitious. Loves money. Status-driven. See right.

Harvey Weinstein

Peter Biskind's book *Down And Dirty Pictures* exposes the Miramax film

DOMESTIC GODDESS MEETS GLOBAL TYRANT

producer as the boss from hell. Now we are not ones to repeat libel willy-nilly, and merely advise you to pick this tome up and acquaint yourself with a red-gulleted monster of movie capitalism.

TONY HUSBAND'S JOKE PAGE

KNOWN TO HIS FRIENDS AS THE WORLD'S WORST JOKE TELLER, TONY HUSBAND ASKS A FEW FAMOUS FACES FOR THEIR FAVOURITE GAGS.

Angus Deayton

Q: What's red and invisible?
A: No tomatoes

John Peel

Q: "What do you do if a bird craps on your windscreen?"
A: "Finish with her"

Neil Kerber

Q: What goes 'ooo'?
A: A cow without any lips
Q: What goes 'aaaa'
A: A sheep without any lips

Jim Poyser

A Mathematician, an architect and an actor enter their dogs in a dog talent show. There's a pile of bones in the ring. The mathematician's dog takes the bones and arranges them so they read 2+2=4. Everyone claps. The architect's dog takes the bones and builds a pyramid out of them. Everyone claps. The actor's dog eats the bones, fucks the other two dogs and then asks for the afternoon off.

Marc (Lard) Riley

A teacher asks her class, "Right children what is a shitsu?"
A little boy puts up his hand. "A zoo without animals, miss.

Keith Allen

A woman texts a man, "My fingers smell of your cock." The man texts back, "well take them out of your arse then"

Rowland Rivron

A man goes to the doctor's, he says "Doctor I'm having hearing problems." The doctor asks, "What are the symptoms?" The man replies, "A cartoon series on Channel 4.'

Noddy Holder

What shoes does a man with two left feet wear?
Flip Flips

Penny Junor

Why did the woman cross the street? That's not the issue, who let her out of the kitchen?

Tony Husband

An Englishman, and Irishman and an American arrive on the viewing deck of the Empire State building. The American stands on the parapet and says, "I'm going to fly round New York and then land back here." He takes off, flies round New York and then lands safely back where he started. The Irishman climbs up on the parapet and says, "Right, I'll do the same." He leaps off the edge and plummets to his death. The Englishman turns to the American and says, "Bleeding hell, you're a bastard when you're pissed, Superman." ◉

GWYN

IDLE PLEASURES: YAWNING

Deliciously contagious but hard to repress in the company of a tedious bore, yawning is nature's way of persuading you to take a break. Close your eyes, sit back and relax as the sensation of sloth envelops your mouth. Inhale luxuriously through your nose as your eyes lightly water and then revel in your impending triumph. Growl out your yawn like a sated lion in the evening sun.

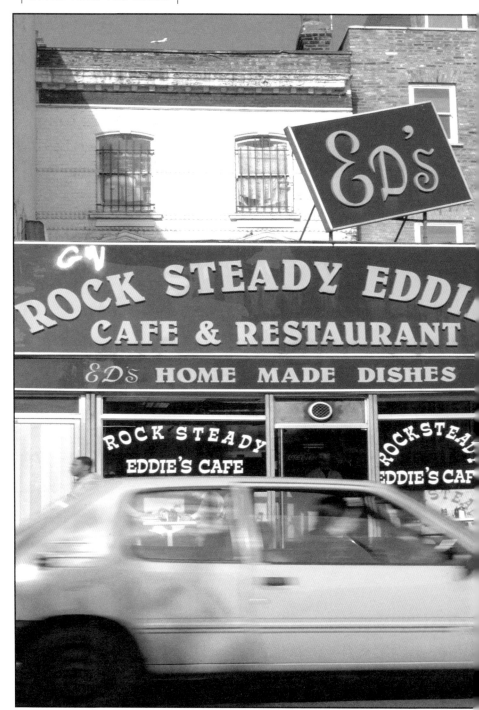

THE JOY OF TAKE-AWAYS

Greg Rowland gets out there.
Photographs by Liz Emerson

There comes a time in a man's life when he becomes restless with the supine ease of the Telephone Delivery and seeks challenges that both deepen and broaden his contact with his fellows. On such occasions, rare as they might be, the notion of actually leaving home to seek out food whispers gently from The Ether. It was Jimi Hendrix who thought that "The Wind Cries Mary". Yet for me it shall always declare "Sweet & Sour Chicken (No. 39)".

And so, for many of us on the Idler's Fundamentalist Wing, who dispense with all pleasures that imply even the most minimal of efforts, whom some call "Lazy Fuckwits", the take-away experience involves a level of commitment more serious than that which we normally prefer to undertake. It is a studied metaphysical exploration — to be out of the home, however briefly, takes that very courage and determination that we find in such short supply.

Thus to bring home the simple cartons, gilded with their stiff cardboard-backed silver foil tops, is to meet the expectations of masculinity since time began. The hunter has returned, stocked with a slightly leaking plastic bag that leaves an indiscriminate puddle on a table when put down injudiciously. He brings with him cartons not just full of delicious food, but packages that epitomise his unbounded love for all humanity.

Let us prepare you then, for this greatest of all Mankind's adventures: wherein food can be won, and hearts can be torn asunder.

We begin with the traditional favourite, the Fish & Chip Shop. Sadly in decline — perhaps due to their doomed affection for the hated Crusty White Roll — a good Fish & Chip shop is hard to find. It is particularly pertinent in the case of this author, who would no sooner eat fish than spend a night of passion with the rotting corpse of Thora Hird, and who is thus wholly dependent on the various chicken and pie offers in such establishments. The rise of the fashionable gourmet Fish & Chip shops, such as The Sea Cow in East Dulwich, is to be noted with much alarm. No chicken has ever set foot nor claw in their shop, yet the sight of the local bourgeoisie waiting — for up to twenty-five minutes — for the delicate ministrations of the undeniably Sapphic counter-staff frying as they wrap their fish with a proud lesbotic dawdle, is a cause of no small amusement as I flounce up the high street towards more poultry fare.

I hurry past Texas Fried Chicken and their foul heresies of southern chicken authenticity. Let me warn you in the strongest possible terms, a visitor to any fried chicken retailer that references any other Southern American State other than Kentucky is playing Russian Roulette with the sundry contents of his stomach and an Offal Vendor's Drib-Drabs. I am also kindly advised by devotees of Sharia Law that these shops' "halal" claims are woefully inaccurate. You have been duly warned.

Nor does the Chicken Cottage tempt me inwards. Although some acquaintances have unkindly claimed that this establishment's name reflects two of my major interests: those of "chicken" and "cottaging". I should like to emphasise that the latter is a calumny based on an unfortunate late-night toilet misunderstanding with a Scottish Gentleman at Scratchwood Services in 1998. Only the briefest of pleasantries were exchanged, I can assure you.

Venturing onwards, we might pass a gaggle of Curry Houses, whose sultry tempting aromas warm the evening air. We are hereby presented with a discourse currently wrestling with the pressures of modernity. A new confident vibrancy has emerged here — names like The Pistachio Club and Indiaah effectively displace the subservient Rajisms of the past.

Moreover, it is surely the case that the history of race relations in this country has been dictated, not so much by a higher moral calling of men, but by the needs of their stomachs. Would Anti-Semitism have retained a foothold in our nation if the Jewish people had brought with them foods other than borscht, gefilte fish and knishes? When a food is as inedible as it is unpronounceable a frightened nation narrows its eyes. Yet the Chinese, Italians and Turks have had far less pubic virulence foisted upon them. Is there not a lesson here for the kindly Albanian and the robust

FOWL HERESY

Romanian? The lesson being: bring something nice to eat to our shores and the middling sensibilities of the Everyman will be no doubt reassured.

Further up the street, on peering through the Kebab Shop I am greeted by stern manly nods of recognition from the tenders of the holy doner. It is a hot, steamy place redolent of the Age Of Industry, where men are men, judged solely by a capacity to consume gallons of chilli sauce. Indeed, it was here that I was once given free chips to celebrate the birth of my first-born boy-child. O happy times!

My journey nears its consummation as I, with considerable trepidation and hushed awe, enter the house of Mr Liu for the very first time.

BRING SOMETHING NICE TO EAT AND THE WORLD WILL LOVE YOU

Before this moment, I have known this place only as an ambient voice for telephone delivery. Yet now I have finally ventured into Shangri-La. Unlike so many Chinese Take-Aways, where the brutal simplicity of the décor gives one no other diversion than watching the proprietor's six-year old daughter perform advanced calculus on the back of a menu, Mr Liu's is a veritable garden of Eden (with no snakes.)

But, like the eponymous mystic from *The Wizard of Oz*, there is no Mr Liu. Nor has there ever been. But there is Bao Chuong, creator of the finest lottery ticket origamis the world has ever seen — a delightful concoction of Western Materialism and Chinese Spirituality. It is he who warmly greets me, takes my order and offers me a prawn cracker as I sit down to ponder the delights the await me in the best place in the world: the Take-Away of the Surrendered Heart. ◉

BRITAIN'S MOST POPULAR TAKE-AWAYS
(SOURCE BY JOSHUA CONSUMER CHECK)

Chinese	31%
Indian	22%
Fish&Chips	11%
KFC	9%
Pizza Hut	7.2%
McDonald's	7%
Burger King	5.2%
Pizza Express	4.5%

SOUP MAN

Bill Drummond is the man with the ladle

You can lose yourself in making soup. The imagination can start to spiral into uncharted regions, reality can become bearable, even enjoyable. You can also find yourself in making soup, though what you find may bore you. It always starts with chopping onions. Holding back the tears has to be mastered, but once that's done, onions are the most rewarding vegetable in the world to chop. Everybody loves the aroma of frying onions. It's what unites all meals in every kitchen around the world.

Earlier this year (2004) I spoke to Sean Kelly, the director of the Cathedral Quarter Arts Festival in Belfast. He wanted to know what I had been up to and I was being my usual evasive self. I mentioned this Soup Line thing I've been thinking about, kind of hoping he might pick up on it.

Things start somewhere.

In 1998 I got an invitation to contribute to an exhibition in Belfast. The exhibition was to be held in a large run-down Victorian town house in the bohemian quarter, if Belfast has such a thing. It was being curated by a pair of artists named Susan Philipsz and Eoghan McTigue who lived in the top floor of the house and operated under the name Grassy Knoll. They were asking every artist type who had ever stayed in the house and was still alive to contribute to the exhibition. I was told that hundreds of artists had stayed there over the years. There were rumours that Oscar Wilde had secret assignations there and every second person you meet in Belfast will tell you that their mother swears blind that Errol Flynn stayed there on more than one occasion. Mark Manning and I spent a few debauched hours there one night in 1996 when we were out promoting our book, *Bad Wisdom*.

I decided that instead of contributing something more recognisably a work of art, I would go over to Belfast and make soup for everybody at this house. I would leave the decision about who the everybody was to the Grassy Knoll. The everybody turned out to be 30-odd Belfast-based artists, cultural contributors and would-be bohemians.

The soup that I made that night was a variation of the one I always make. I call it Big Pan Soup. The only fixed ingredient is onions, after that anything I can get hold of and that makes me think, "Yeah, that will add something," goes in. Along with hunks of bread and chunks of cheese the soup is a meal in itself.

The evening was a riotous success, wine flowed, songs were sung and there was plenty of washing up to do. Over the next few days I documented the whole thing in a story called "Making Soup". The quote at the beginning of this story comes from it.

In the autumn of 2002 I took part in a live art festival in Nottingham called NOW. I was doing a performance thing that came out of my book *How To Be An Artist*, and in connection with this I wrote a piece in the local listings magazine, *City Lights*. Originally it was supposed to be an interview. They emailed me a list of questions but I found the questions impossible to answer. So instead I wrote about why this was and then offered up the questions to readers. Whoever emailed me back with the best answers to the questions would get the prize of me coming around to their place to make them, their family and close friends soup. Only one person responded, so I judged her the winner. She was called Julz.

On a wet cold February night in 2003, I drove up to Nottingham with an address BluTacked to the dashboard and my soup-making utensils in the back of the Land Rover. The house turned out to be a red-brick, two-up two-down terrace. I bought all the ingredients from an Asian greengrocers at the corner of the street. I got to work chopping onions in the cramped but spotless kitchen and by the time the soup was ready the place was rammed with her family and close friends. They were a raucous lot, and the cliché motley crew could be used to describe them.

I got out of the house with all my bits and bobs before midnight. Down the M1 and I was sitting in the silence of my kitchen with a mug of tea by 2am. And as I was supping the tea I was thinking that it had been a weird but brilliant evening. There seemed to be something about turning up at a stranger's house and doing this communal thing with a bunch of people you have never met before. I was staring at a map of the British Isles that we have stuck on the larder door. I started to imagine a straight line all the way across the map joining Belfast and

NOTICE

Take a map of the British Isles. Draw a straight line diagonally across the map so that it cuts through Belfast and Nottingham.

If your home is on this line, contact soupline@penkiln-burn.com

Arrangements will then be made for Bill Drummond to visit and make one vat of soup for you, your family, and your close friends.

fb Poster 54   2003

There was nothing on the flyer that explained who the fuck I was or if it was art or just some weird form of charity

Nottingham. Then I had an idea. It was a simple one and it went like this: the line is called The Soup Line and anyone who lives on it has the right to contact me and invite me around to their place to make soup for them, their family and close friends.

Anyway, this is what Sean had to say.

"So this sounds interesting, Bill. How's it been going so far?"

"Well I haven't actually been out there doing it yet. It's still in the fantasy stage, but I have done a couple of my posters, one with a list of instructions on how to find out if you live on The Soup Line and what to do if you do. The other poster is a recipe, in case you want to make a rough approximation of the soup yourself. I've also made one of my text paintings with the words MAKE SOUP on it."

"So Bill, would you be up for coming over for the festival at the back end of April, making soup along the length of The Soup Line that cuts across the north of Ireland?"

"Yes," I said.

Yesterday – 2 May 2004 – I got back from a week in Ireland, and today I'm trying to work out what it is I've been doing other than make soup for people I have never met before. In some twisted way, it was one of the most creatively rewarding weeks of my life.

A fortnight before I drove the long drive up to Stranraer from my place, to get the ferry across to Belfast I put together an A5 flyer. On one side was a reduced version of the poster telling you what to do if you live on The Soup Line that I mentioned above (Penkiln Burn Poster 54) on the other a map of the north of Ireland with The Soup Line across it and the names of the towns and villages that it cuts through printed in bold. Sean Kelly had these flyers sent off to libraries, post offices and other likely locations in the town and villages along the line. In the corner of the map side of the flyer was this: *Bill Drummond will be based in Belfast between 30 April and 6 May 2004 as part of the Cathedral Quarter Arts Festival, constructing the Irish section of The Soup Line. Every evening he will be available to travel to one home situated on The Soup Line and make soup. If asked "Why?" he is likely to say, "Because it is a friendly thing to do." Bill Drummond comes equipped with ingredients and utensils. The selected host is expected to provide liquid refreshments and a warm welcome. If you live on the line and would like Bill Drummond to come to your home and make soup for you, your family and friends; email soupline@penkilnburn.com or contact the Festival office on info@cqaf.com or on the telephone 028 902 324 23.*

There was nothing on the flyer that explained who the fuck I was or if it was art or just some weird form of charity. The response was instant, but as I planned to make soup only once in each place along the line I had to draw names from a hat and turn down the vast majority of the invitations. Things got complicated, as they tend to do, and I ended up doing lunchtimes as well on most days, so I made eleven soups in only six days. What was great for me was the variety of places where I ended up making soup. I could be at a residential care home for the elderly at lunchtime and a condemned house full of debauched students in the evening.

I have a habit of writing in my head as I am driving, and for much of the eight hours' drive south from Stranraer to my house I was writing about straight lines on maps and how I had always been taken by the fact that a bunch of men in London or somewhere would have a map of a distant land and rule a line across the map and decide that forever more what lies on one side is Egypt and on the other Libya or draw the line between Kazakhstan and Uzbekistan or even the parallel that divides Canada from the USA and what I was writing in my head usually doesn't have any full stops and sentences would just go on and on... these lines will be the deciding factor, come wartime, on which side a young man will give his life.

I like the idea that I have taken a map and drawn a line on it and decided to give it a name and make up rules about it. "I'm afraid it states quite clearly here, that if you don't live bang on the line Bill Drummond will not come and make soup at your place." It's not about living to the north, south, east or west of this line, you've got to live right on it. I suppose it must have something of the ley line business about it, except I hate all that Celtic myth, new age stuff. Ley lines have no mystical or spiritual powers other than those we invest in them. Just 'cause some blokes 3,000 years ago decided to build their stone circles in a particular place doesn't give it any more value than a line drawn across any part of the world.

Well, that was the sort of stuff that I was writing in my head last night and I was hoping to get it a bit more focused today but I think it is better leaving it unfocused. Trying to nail down why the idea of The Soup Line excites me might just kill it off. I just know that it does and for some reason those people that I have met along it have accepted the notion of this line very positively, in public anyway. One person reminded me of the Stone Soup fable; a couple told me that the phrase "taking the soup" has a very negative connotation for one camp in the Irish sectarian divide; and two or three commented on the blind trust that had to exist for both parties in allowing a strange man into your house under the pretext he is going to make you, your family and close friends soup.

I haven't quite worked out how I can justify it to my family. Can't see how it is going to put bread on the table. The obvious thing to do would be to write about what happened at the different homes that I visited along the line. But if I did that and ended up publishing it, I would somehow feel that I was exploiting the welcome I had been given.

This morning there was an email from *Richard and Judy* wanting me to go on their show to talk about The Soup Line. There was another from a BBC TV producer who was interested in discussing the possibility of developing a whole Soup Line thing into a TV series. I can't deny that there was a part of me that went, "I'm on to a fuckin' winner here." Then I thought about my previous brushes with TV and how shite they had all been and how they had reduced whatever I had been doing to the lowest common denominator. And I remembered what my colleague Cally told me, "Bill, *soup* is the medium." And I said, "You're fuckin' right, Cally, the *soup* is the medium." I didn't know what he meant and I don't know where that leaves the message but it sounded good to me. ●

HOW FORMS WORK

Edward Bicycle reveals a few bureaucratic mysteries to Ian Vince

As Secretary of State for Fiscal Discipline at the Indolent Revenue, I get many letters everyday. Many of them seek my official intervention to correct some pecuniary dysfunction or other. Others are from regional newspapers, appealing for information about the tax affairs of local socialists and other long-haired guttersnipes up to no good.

The rest of my correspondence is almost entirely made up of earnest requests, asking me why there are so many forms to fill in and how the Indolent Revenue can help you, the generic face in the crowd, to lead a more efficient and formless existence.

Well, I'm afraid that it's unlikely to change soon.

Forms are part of the British Way of Life. They play a vital role in the social fabric of these islands. The official form is as much a part of etiquette as the strict alignment of Extended Silver Service for diplomatic functions. I often recount the tale of one Foreign Office dinner where the Brûlée Paddle was laid on the wrong side of the Joss Stick of Xanthes. It is an easy mistake, but one which would have signalled war were it not for the precise alignment of the soup bowl with the cayenne pepper pot.

In terms of British decorum, forms are as important as that potentially misplaced pepper pot. If it were not for the officially codified exchange of information between citizen and state, we would be no better than lawless savages acting on whims of the moment. We need an objective and measurable communication system. The alternative would simply be lacking in precision or clarity and only the most extreme messages – gushing love letters, for instance, or a Jiffy bag of faeces – would convey the subjective fancy of the correspondent.

But it's not about collecting information in order to oppress you in a scientific manner. It's about so much more than that.

Your P-45, for example, leads a very interesting life the moment it leaves your sweaty hand and enters the bureaucratic domain. While you worry about your mortgage payment and the scowling, unsymmetrical faces of staff at your local Jobcentrehassleplus, your P-45 begins the kind of exotic journey only pre-packaged oriental snacks can dream of.

Your data is first inputted into an air-conditioned computer silo for processing, dispersal and retrieval. After sorting, data re-alignment and qualified re-dispersal, the original P-45 is sent to Rangoon for I-Ching interpretation by accountants at the As Above, So Below Institute of Tax.

After three full moons have elapsed, the original form is burnt in a sealed bell jar and the carbonised remains are collected for auditing and mass-spectrometry. The jar is then broken against the hull of a ship bearing your National Insurance records which is then sailed into the Bermuda Triangle for processing. You can find a fuller description of the process in the Tax Office leaflet "What the Fuck Have You Done With My Tax Records?", which is freely available at your local Office inside a large rotating jar of wasps. ◉

Indolent Revenue

Hooray, you've been fired.
Copy for dole-draining scum

P45t 1t

For the employer

- *Please fill this form in as you laugh maniacally within earshot of remaining staff furtively cowering in their cubicles.*
- *It will take approximately 0.7 Havana Cigar to complete in full.*
- *You may photocopy and pin this form to a staff noticeboard for the purposes of employee oppression.*

1 Employee ID Chip #

This is often located in a small cavity behind the employee's left ear.

2 Place employee teardrop on treated strip.
We need to confirm that your employee interprets your complex use of management euphemisms as dismissal.

3 Bullshit checklist:

Enabling blue-sky platforms for alternative personal growth

Re-focussing Human Resources

Responding to a bijou personnel paradigm

For the employee

1 Reason for your dismissal:

- Gross Idealism
- Tested positive for Soul
- Evacuating your colon on your Line Manager's in-tray.
- Tactless flair for your job
- Too popular and likeable

2 Please confirm you have read these clauses in your contract before you rip it up in a final pointless gesture of defiance.

- I agree that my pension fund contributions may be temporarily re-allocated to the 4.30 at Haydock Park.
- To counter office stationery theft, sniffer dogs sensitive to the aroma of post-it notes will be deployed at building exits.
- In the event of my dismissal, Maoist disavowal and character assassination will form part of the company's grieving process.

★ About this form

Detach this form from your forehead and hand it to your new leader.

You may need this form at an indeterminate time in the middle-future when your tax affairs are investigated by a consortium of spiteful paper-pushing gits in polyester suits and Ford Mondeos.

Please read the notes attached to Part 9 of sub-section B of this and **all other** forms. It will explain what to do next in a patronising, yet vaguely threatening and authoritarian, manner.

You are not alone.

To the new employer

Hello. My name is

I come from

Please find me a desk and sap my soul for the next [   ] day/month/year *

* This footnote left intentionally blank.

For office use only wheeeeeeeeeeee

THE TRUTH

In his latest column, Brian Dean accuses government and media of exaggerating the extent and dangers of obesity

Obesity has risen by almost 400% in 25 years according to a report from the Commons Health Select Committee. The national growth in waistlines could, we're told, have the following consequences:
• Children will die before their parents
• There will be a huge demand for kidney dialysis
• There will be many more blind people (Reported in the *Guardian*, 27/5/04).
The media lapped this up, of course – it's instant headline material. In fact, there's been an alarming rise in gratuitous health-scare headlines over the past twelve months. For example:
• "0Scottish farmed salmon is full of cancer toxins" (*Telegraph*, Jan 2004)
• "What's in your dinner? PCBs, dioxins, pesticides" (*Daily Mail*, Jan 2004)
• "Bird flu could be worse than Sars" (*Times*, Jan 2004)
• "Coffee drinking linked to higher miscarriage risk" (*Telegraph*, Oct 2003)
• "Official: Atkins diet can be deadly" (*Observer*, Aug 2003)

Moral Panic

It's the same old scaremongering. The obesity scare fits the definition of "moral panic" given by sociologist Stanley Cohen in 1972: "A condition... emerges to become defined as a threat to societal values and interests; its nature is presented in a stylized and stereotypical fashion by the mass media; the moral barricades are manned by editors, bishops, politicians and other right-thinking people; socially accredited experts pronounce their diagnoses and solutions." You'd assume there's good scientific evidence that weight loss is medically beneficial. But according to Paul Campos (author of *The Obesity Myth*), there's no such evidence. It's true that severe obesity has been correlated with ill health, but it doesn't automatically follow that losing weight is good for everyone defined as "overweight".

Steven Milloy, of JunkScience.com, claims that "reported correlations between overweight/obesity and premature death don't inspire even minimal confidence until the obesity in question is extreme."

Government-approved body weight Your BMI (Body Mass Index, calculated from height and weight) shows if you're "overweight". BMI categories have recently changed, resulting in millions of people becoming "overweight" or "obese" overnight. Here are some well-known fatties, according to BMI categories: Brad Pitt: "overweight"; Mel Gibson: "overweight"; George Bush: "overweight"; Russell Crowe: "obese"; George Clooney "obese"; Tom Cruise: "obese" (*Observer*, 30/5/04; *Guardian*, 24/4/04).

Junk Science

In 1996, a US study on body weight (by the National Centre for Health Statistics) analysed data from 600,000 subjects. The mortality rate for white non-smokers in the supposedly ideal BMI range (ie thin) was the same as for those in the overweight range. Dozens of medical studies have found increasing body weight to be associated with a lower incidence of various cancers. Heavier women have much lower rates of osteoporosis (in Britain, more women die from osteoporosis-related hip fracture than from breast, cervical and uterine cancer combined).
(Source: *Guardian* 24/4/04)

We're already eating less

The food intake of the average Briton has actually decreased by 750 calories a day over the past 30 years, according to a study by the Royal College of General Practitioners. (The current official recommendation for calorie intake is 2,000 a day for women and 2,500 for men). The reason we're getting fatter is supposedly because we are burning off 800 fewer calories a day than we were in the 1970s. "Children today don't walk anywhere. They go by car", says a *Daily Mail* editorial, echoing widespread media disapproval of sedentary lifestyles. The *Daily Mail*, of course, is well-known for playing down the risks (such as crime) of walking on Britain's streets.
(Sources: *Daily Telegraph*, 30/5/04; *Daily Mail*, 27/5/04)

The War on Fat

The obesity scare, like the WMD scare, seems to be an American import. Paul Campos says: "The war on fat is both a cause and a consequence of the transformation of the Protestant work ethic into the American diet ethic... what the American élites consider most desirable is a body whose appearance signals a triumph of the will over desire itself." Obesity is an ideal health scare as:
• It confirms the views of puritan control-freaks
• It keeps awkward stories off the news
• It creates a lucrative pharmaceutical market
• It correlates with poverty ("poor = ignorant/lazy")

Fat worse than death

An *Esquire* magazine poll of 1,000 women between the ages of 18 and 25 showed that 54% would rather be run over by a truck than be fat. The diet industry is worth billions. There's enormous social pressure to be thin – without health scares. The medical warnings just add new anxieties to existing anxieties.
(*Esquire*, Feb. 1994)

Food Anxiety

If each mouthful of food makes you anxious (calories kill, after all), consider the following: a pound of body fat contains 3,500 calories. A large bar (100g) of chocolate contains about 500 calories. So if you stuff your face with chocolate (in addition to what you normally eat) every day for a whole week, you'll gain, at most, one pound in weight.

Five portions a day

We've been urged to eat more fruit and vegetables because they contain antioxidants, compounds that ward off oxidation and prevent heart disease. Chocolate comes from fruit (the cocoa bean is the fruit of the cacao tree) and is a good source of antioxidants – make sure you get five daily portions.
Brian Dean runs anxietyculture.com

THE FINE LINE BETWEEN

BEING EMPLOYED

BEING EXPERIMENTED UPON

FROM RAT RACE TO LAB RAT

BEING EMPLOYED	BEING EXPERIMENTED UPON
Meeting	Placebo
Cubicles	Cages
Suit and tie	Whole body shave
New management theory	New surgical techniques
Hard day's graft	Ear grafted on your back
We clock on at 8	We hit the red button with our beaks at 8
Timesheet	Behavioural maze
Pret A Manger	Pavlov and his dogs
Salary	Maze cheese
P45	Carbon dioxide euthanasia chamber
Boss asks you out to dinner	Lab assistant with the cold hands
Co-workers weeping in the toilets	Dogs with electrodes attached to their brain howling at shadows
Raddled, bitter middle age staff	Dead-eyed grey-haired monkey with missing scalp

THE FINE LINE

JOHN RIORDAN

MDA

ON BEING 17

The laziest days of your life, says Edward Cumming

It is frequently declared by bothersome elders that our schooldays are the best of our lives. I have always been aware of having a vaguely enjoyable time in life, but recently the *Idler* has made me realise why this is; adolescence, one's "serious" time at school, also happens to be one of the best times to be idle. I would think possibly even better than university.

School offers some great opportunities for idling, and I would suggest that schooldays offer a microcosm of what the adult culture could become with some more mass idling. Firstly, nobody works more than four hours a day. If you smoke, rather than being martyred, as is the case in the stuffy, grown-up working environment, you are genuinely still a bit cooler than those who don't. Harder drugs and laziness are treated with similar respect. Shagging loads of good-looking people in a short space of time is a sign of talent, rather than any moral weakness. In fact, everything which responsible people frown upon aged twenty-three plus is encouraged by adolescents. One only has to cast an eye around the teenage idols from any generation to see that the most respected are often those who do least. From Elvis, who died in that laziest of ways, eating while on the loo, to current porridge-eating crack-smoking favourite Pete Doherty, through Jack "peanut butter sandwiches to keep it up" Nicholson and the spectacular Henry Miller, via, of course, Withnail, great teenage role models are often remarkably slothful. In my year, the most popular people are almost without exception those who have been most often in detention; it is not simply the "edge" they are given that makes this the case. They simply know better how to have a good time.

The obvious counter to all this is that one's schooldays are merely the poor cousins of time spent at university, indeed all of the arguments I've outlined above seem pretty much valid as a student too, but I would argue that this is not the case. At university one has responsibilities. You have to work for yourself, rather than having everything plonked down in front of you. Laundry and food is not sorted out by free domestic help (parents). More often than not one has to earn petty cash by working. Together with this is the dawning "maturity" which dictates a movement towards more work, with sights on future life. The element of rebellion which ought to accompany the best idling is also lost when one becomes a proper student. It is expected that a student will sleep in until two o'clock on a Monday afternoon, whereas doing this while working a 9 to 4 school day retains a certain amount of rebellious satisfaction, without it ever having any serious repercussions. Similarly, one can have a nap during double history and make an idle statement, in the way that a conventional siesta, on one's own time, does not. And what's more, at the end of the day, it's the parents who still pay for the trip to the pub.

It is perhaps university when most people awake to the possibilities of idling, but this is because they have been blinded during their schooldays prime by

EDWIN MARNEY

the illusion of pressure created by exams. School happens at the perfect age for laziness; old enough to drink and smoke and take drugs and make love under a lotus tree, but at the same time not old enough to have any moral qualms or physical side effects. At seventeen I still find it hard to get a serious hangover, no matter how much I drink. Nobody cares if I sit in a chair rather than going out of a Saturday; in fact some of my friends and I have begun an anti-clubbing movement on the grounds of a few incontrovertible truths: firstly none of us can dance; secondly (possibly as a consequence) we rarely pull in clubs; thirdly you can't have a conversation; fourthly it's farcically expensive; fifthly we'd all rather be in bed by 4am and finally we'd all rather pass the time in the pub. On paper it is such a convincing argument that I'm rather surprised that there isn't an idler-wide ban on clubbing: it seems to me the

fusser's evening pastime of choice, beaten in this regard possibly only by speed-dating, or shot-downing competitions.

Even the little work that school provides these days seems geared towards the sloth. Coursework, which is increasingly important, can be bought off the internet with no trouble at all. Even supposed essay subjects are becoming more and more about factual recall, and learning facts is the ultimate idler "work". How many other official tasks can be conducted through a Walkman in a hammock in some exotic clime?

It is a duty of the elder idlers out there to inform the nation's youth, who are probably too busy doing nothing to read the literature themselves, that they are failing to appreciate what are indeed the best days of their lives, because for two or three years there are almost unlimited possibilities for being idle. ◉

THE GIRO PLAYBOY

We present selections from the
Giro Playboy, issues one to six.
Words and pictures by Michael Smith

For a while I lived in a seaside resort, in a bargain bedsit next to the King of Portugal's old mansion retreat, in "The Beverly Hills of the Georgian era"... nowadays it's a faded bohemia of trannies and longhair public school bongo players and midget scousers gouching in telephone boxes next to the methadone clinic... I would get up at 2 o'clock and wander around restlessly in flip flops, on my giro holiday, smiling at the beautiful scenery, feeling useless, wondering what my role could be in this world... that boring beautiful ocean just stretching out before me everyday, as I pondered what to do... doing nothing seemed like some religious ordeal in that place... that town had a mystical quality about it; I remember when the mists would roll in and the sunsets would become completely diffused in the fog; the whole town would be drenched in misty rose, the buildings in the distance disappeared, and the grand old dreamy Pier seemed to fade into a rosy void, as if this were a town built on the edge of eternity, the last outpost before the Ever After...

I tried to get a job as the driver on this miniature Victorian train that ran up and down the prom, but they gave it to a guy who fit the bill better, a chubby little bald guy who looked like the fat controller off Thomas the Tank Engine... I didn't get the job in the cemetery where Aleister Crowley was buried either... even the menial jobs there had a dream like quality... it was like living in a place that was stuck in a dream of itself... clotted cream Regency hotels dreaming of themselves as the sun set over the sea... the fairy lights twinkling along the prom in the evening... the 24 hour gay greasy spoons and the drifters building bonfires on the beach... but behind all the magic was this nagging sense of pointlessness... it was just so blissful and dreamlike that nobody could ever get anything done... nothing in that town was tangible, it just shimmered like a mirage with its fairy lights floating along the coast, mesmerising you into its magical limbo...

After a while my sister left and then the gallery shut down, and I was all alone in that strange town, and loneliness and isolation began to make me strange, too... days and days spent inside a room, with occasional shopping forays and restless walks... one night it had got late and I was painting, but the domestic coziness I'd felt with my sister around was gone; this time round it was as if that same room were locked in the heart of a mountain, or isolated in an airtight Lunar module, and out the window you could perhaps see the coldness of space, and then the blue

Earth twinkling in the distance, and you yearned for it and its life, but the distance was just too far, so you had to stay cocooned in the lonely room... and this was the situation I was trying to paint myself out of, but the painting just ended up as a manifestation of all of this... the painting was a sinister looking depiction of a Victorian séance... it was a deep gloomy blue colour except for some shadowy heads and the big circle of hands in the middle that were joined as a bridge to the world of the dead... the painting all of a sudden started doing my head in, and I had the creeping sensation I was doing something I shouldn't, that the very act of painting this séance was a way of meddling with unseen forces and opening myself up to them... my back was now up and I felt quite freaked out... there was no curtain and the big bay window was exposed to the vast blackness of the night... I tried not to look out of it but it kept troubling my peripheral vision... and then in a horrible split second my arse nearly fell out when I caught a fleeting glimpse of a human shaped shadow flapping its giant bat wing near the fire escape! Trying to bring myself back down, I kept telling myself this was just my imagination, and everything was fine, but then I would catch sight of that big thing again... I had to put the picture outside the room... and lying in bed that night absolutely shitting myself I think I prayed to God (who I don't normally believe in) to watch over my soul... a few weeks later a friend was visiting for the weekend and we were up late quite spangled when my friend's little eyes started looking worried... when I asked what the matter was they reluctantly said there was a shadowy human shape flapping its bat wing near the fire escape... at this point I stopped being scared and decided enough was enough... I got angry and started shouting "Fuck off, Bat Wing!"... who did Bat Wing think it was anyway, turning up uninvited to do my head in? I decided not to take anymore shit off ghosts... after that night, when ever I got a bit scared I'd just psyche myself up and mutter at Bat Wing to fuck off... and I guess that's just what happens to people who live alone in bedsits in strange towns...

Sitting on that empty beach with nothing to do, I'd draw little pictures on the pebbles, little pictures about my life... and when they were done I'd just leave them there, and maybe someone would find them, and maybe they wouldn't, and they'd just sit there on the beach undiscovered forever, like me... and as miserable as I was I'd find strange consolation in certain things, like the Giant Tomato ride looking all derelict and abandoned off-season, or the waves, or the sunset turning everything a Devonshire cream... I remember one evening looking for the biggest pebble on the beach, and then looking for the littlest, and then realizing the biggest one had a hole in it that was exactly the same size as the littlest one, and that the littlest one fit into it snug as a nut, and finding some strange consolation and wonder in that, in the suggestion of some secret law of harmony in the world, and things being connected and in their place, even if it didn't seem to be panning out that way for me... ✒

THE GIRO
PLAYBOY

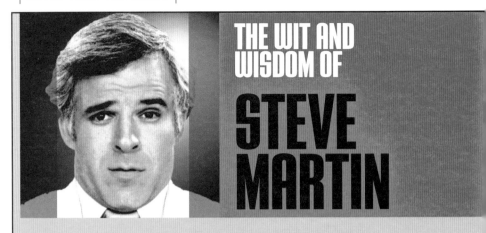

THE WIT AND WISDOM OF
STEVE MARTIN

The Society Of the Preservation Of Comedy Genius presents Steve Martin, the world's funniest white man, in "Homage to Steve!" The following are lovingly culled from Steve's stand-up albums *A Wild And Crazy Guy*, *Let's Get Small* and more

What Steve Believes

I believe in rainbows and puppy dogs and fairy tales.

And I believe in the family – Mom and Dad and Grandma... and Uncle Todd who waves his penis.

And I believe in eight of the Ten Commandments.

And I believe in going to church every Sunday unless there's a game on.

And I believe that sex is one of the most beautiful, wholesome and natural things that money can buy.

And I believe it's derogatory to refer to a woman's breasts as boobs, jugs, Winnebagos or golden bozos, and you should only refer to them as hooters.

And I believe you should place a woman on a pedestal – high enough so you can look up her dress.

And I believe in Equality. Equality for everyone – no matter how stupid they are or how much better I am than they are.

And people think I'm crazy for believing this, but I believe robots are stealing my luggage.

And I believe I made a mistake when I bought a thirty storey one-bedroom apartment.

And I believe Ronald Reagan can make this country what it once was – an Arctic region covered with ice.

And I believe the United States should allow all foreigners in this country provided they can speak our native language... Apache.

Steve on Drugs #1

I'm on drugs. I mean, you know what it is – it's the deal, man. I like to... get small. It's a wi-i-i-ild, wi-i-i-illd drug. Very dangerous for kids, though, because they get really small. I know I shouldn't get small when I'm driving but, er, I was driving around the other day and a cop pulls me over. And he goes, "Heyyy, are yew small?" I said, "No, I'm tall, I'm tall!" He said, "Well, I'm gonna have to measure you." He had a little test they give you – it's a balloon. If you can get inside of it... they know... you're small. One night I got really small and got inside a vacuum cleaner... and the drug wore off. I retained the shape of a vacuum cleaner for about two weeks. Wi-i-i-ild ... to get... smalllll.

Steve's Roots

You say to me, "Steve, how did you get your start? Was it easy for you on the way up?" No. I started off on the bottom. I was born a poor black child. And all day long around the house I would sing the blues. But then I heard my first Mantovani record and then I knew that this was where it was at for me; this is the kind of music I enjoy. These are my people. So I decided to become white. I had my cock shortened and then I got a job as a television weatherman.

Steve's Smoke

It doesn't bother me in a nightclub 'cos I'm used to it, but if I'm in a restaurant and I'm eating and someone says, "Heyyy, mind if I smooooke?" I say, "No. Mind if I fart? It's one of my habits. Yeah, they got a special section for me on airplanes now. I quit once for a year, you know, but I gained a lot of weight. It's hard to quit. After sex I really have the urge to light one up."

Steve and Materialism

I'm into bread. I love money. I love everything about money – I love to eat it. Eat money... They say you can't take it with you? I'm taking it with me. I'm into bread. I loooove bread. I bought some pretty good stuff. Got me a $300 pair of socks. I got a fur sink... an electric dog-polisher... gasoline-powered turtleneck

sweater. And, of course, I bought some dumb stuff, too.

Steve's Dietary Requirements

A lot of people say to me, "Hey, you travel around all the time, you must not be able to get good foods to eat," but I love hotdogs and you can get a hotdog any place so it's easy for me to eat right. But people still come up and say, "Ohh, don't eat hotdogs, there's really weird things in 'em," but that doesn't bother me 'cos I love animal lips. And rat faeces is about one of my favourite things, I guess.

Steve's Ambitions

I've finally figured out my goals in life, and this is the important thing. This is what I am doing. You see, the important thing in knowing your goals is not to set some big impossible goal that you can never reach; you've got to have a series of smaller goals that you can accomplish and get the reward and move on to the next one. This is what I've done. My goal now? I want to be the All Being Master Of Time, Space And Dimension. Then I wanna go to Europe.

Steve and Maturity

I like getting older. I thought I wouldn't but life is easier as you get older because you become prejudiced. Because you've dealt with things. Not against race or anything, it's just about things – because you've dealt with them before and you know it's going to be boring and you just close the door – (makes noise of giant iron door slamming shut) BFFFFFFFF! People come up and go, "Hey! Let's go try this NEW THING!!" – KKKKHHHHH! Sorry. We're closed. I think the secret to enjoying getting older is to be able to be honest with yourself, because there are certain changes that do take place as you get older and they are nothing to be ashamed of, and this is what I have learned. For example, I know that some day my hair will turn grey, and when that happens I know I will be able to accept it because I am honest with myself.

Steve's Artistic Integrity

I'm going back to the old traditional comedy bits. I know I used to do the Far Out but now I'm back to the traditional – because I have them both now, the traditional on the one hand, the Far Out on the other. So now, the Whole, the Unified... Because this appeals to everyone. This way you don't eliminate, and I think if you appeal to everyone it's more... money.

Steve's Possessions

I feel good tonight, I really do. I finally got something I always wanted and that's important. It really is. I finally got some hostages. Well, you see so many people with hostages nowadays, and you say, "Hey! I'd like some, too!" So I got three of them, they're really nice people, we're getting along great. They're tied in a sack outside at the top of the flagpole, and I'm gonna blow 'em up at midnight, too, unless, of course, I get my threeeeee demaaaaaands: A hundred thousand in cash, getaway car, and I want the letter M stricken from the English language. You see, you've always got to make one crazy demand. That way, if you're caught, you can plead insanity... (Chuckles to himself:) Ha ha ha! Getaway car...!

Steve's Sophistication, Intellectual-Wise

I'm into the sophisticated kinda thing 'cos I went to college and studied

Philosophy and Psychology. I'm pretty proud of that. How many people studied Philosophy at college? See, they can never raise their hand more than halfway 'cos they're so confused after about two years.

I studied the great philosophers – So Crates, Plateau. You learn the important things [in Philosophy]. Like, if you study Geology, which is all facts, as soon as you get out of school you forget it all, because it's all numbers and things. But with Philosophy you remember just enough to screw you up for the rest of your life. You study all the important ethical questions, like, "Is it OK to yell 'Movie!' in a crowded firehouse?" Religious questions – "Does the Pope shit in the woods?"

It's so hard to believe in anything anymore, you know what I mean? It's like Religion – you can't take it seriously because it seems so mythological and seems so arbitrary, and then on the other hand science is pure empiricism and, by virtue of its method, it excludes metaphysics. I guess I wouldn't believe in anything if it wasn't for my Lucky Astrology Mood Watch.

Steve on Drugs #2

I'm not into drugs, I don't mess around with that stuff. I used to, I'll have to be honest with you. But in the old days, y'know, everybody'd get stoned, y'know, and the whole audience'd be stoned. I'd walk out stoned... and people'd be watching me and they'd be going (imitates huge toke on spliff), "Hey, those guys are priddy good." They come up to me after the show: "You guys were great, man. Hey, wanna smoke some shit?" - No. – "C'mon, smoke some shit. Go ahead." – Naw, I don't want any marijuana. – "Marijuana? This is shit. I am smoking my own shit."

Steve's Love Code

That's a myth about entertainers – you always think they meet a lot of girls on the road but it's not true, because you come in to town for one night, you don't get time to get to know anybody, and I'm not into that One Night thing. I think a person should get to know someone and even be in love with them before you use and degrade them.

Steve's Linguistic Mastery

I've got a book coming out, I'm pretty proud of that. It's a serious work and I hope you pick it up. It's called *How To Get Along With Everyone*. I didn't write it by myself. I wrote it with this other asshole jerk-off.

Language is my thing, being a comedian. If you don't have a command of language, it's nothing to be embarrassed about. But this is my profession and, let's face it, some people have a way with words; other people, er... oh, not have way.

Steve and Art

I've had a good time since I've been in San Francisco. There's so much. An intellectual town – and I'm certainly into that. Did I tell you I went to the Turd Museum? They've got some great shit there. I guess some of that crap's worth a lot of money, too.

Steve's Final Thought

I gotta get going now but I would like to remind you of something the great Maharishi Guru taught me over fifteen years ago. Maharishi was a close personal friend of mine and I studied with him for fifteen long, long boring years. I didn't really learn that much but the day I was leaving the Maharishi said something to me I've never forgotten. The Maharishi said, "ALWAYS - !" Wait: It was, "NEVER!" No: "Always take a litterbag in your car. It doesn't take up much room and if it gets full you can just toss it out the window."
We recommend his book, Pure Drivel ◉

THE IDLE COOK

A SLOW TURKEY by Rowley Leigh

aul Bocuse is the godfather of French haute cuisine. It was Paul who produced the famous *consommé* of foie gras and truffles under a puff pastry dome that so delighted President Giscard d'Estaing at the Elysee Palace. Bocuse is in the great tradition, in a line of direct descent through the even more legendary Ferdinand Point (a real chef, tipping the scale at 24 stone and endowed with a Churchillian appetite for champagne and Cote Rotie) and a tradition stretching back to the great eminences, Escoffier, Urban Dubois, Gouffe and back to the great codifier himself, Antonin Careme. Bocuse is still there, at Collonges Mont d'Or, on the outskirts of Lyons, and is still presiding over a restaurant obdurately producing his classics, such as the aforesaid *consommé*, the sea bass filled with lobster mousse, the cardoons with beef marrow and the crayfish and truffle gratin. Although a giant, he was left behind in the glory days of nouvelle cuisine, dismissed as a fossil by the prophets and proselytisers for that now defunct movement. His food was rich and old fashioned and hopelessly traditional in an era when kiwi fruit, raspberry vinegar and fromage frais were the buzz ingredients of the decade and water was hailed as the key to making a good sauce.

Bocuse's cookbook was always a key text for me. Such dishes as partridge with cabbage and bacon, real pike quenelles, petits pois *à la francaise* and salmis of woodcock, among countless other classics that I really wanted to learn to cook properly, came alive under his guidance. Beyond this canon of was a slightly anarchic strain of gastronomic wit. There were recipes so stunning in their conception and gorgeously, deeply impractical for a young chef commuting

1.) Get Turkey
2.) Stuff with truffles
3.) Stuff with sausagemeat
4.) Put in a big sack
5.) Dig a hole & bury it

CHLOE KING

between Shepherds Bush and the City of London. These are the dishes that I especially commend to the idle cook, to those people who are prepared to spend two or three days over a dish, to embark on a voyage of gastronomic discovery every bit as important as its eventual result. There is the famous *lièvre de Senator Coutoux* that is braised over several days in a combination of goose fat, pork fat and Chambertin – at least five years old and from a reputable grower – before the sauce is thickened with a mixture of fine old brandy and the hare's blood and liver. There is the soup cooked inside a pumpkin, the ham braised in hay and, an especial favourite of mine, the leg of beef cooked over an open flame ("turn slowly for twelve hours...").

With Christmas in mind, a delightfully simple recipe for the much maligned turkey commends itself. The health and safety police will recommend refrigeration in preference to the garden sod.

TURKEY WITH TRUFFLES

Take a turkey of four to six pounds. Stuff it with a pound of sausage meat and the same amount of sliced truffles. Slide some truffle slices under the skin before trussing the bid. Wrap your turkey in wax paper and enclose it in a potato sack in the soil of your garden, dig a hole, not too deep and bury the turkey. The cold and the humidity of the earth will allow the aroma of the truffles to come out fully. Two days later, prepare a courtbullion with carrots, celery, onions, leeks, cloves, salt, pepper, a veal shin, and an oxtail cut into pieces. Poach your turkey for one and a half hours. Serve with vegetables. ✆

HISTORY OF THE PASTY

Edward Sage salutes Cornish cuisine

A PASTY IN HAND IS WORTH TWO IN A SHOP

and Enide", contains the first textual reference to pasties: "Next Guivret opened a chest and took out two pasties. 'My friend,' says he, 'now try a little of these cold pasties.'" Both characters came from parts of what today is Cornwall.

In the thirteenth and fourteenth centuries the pasty was filled with venison, beef, lamb, salmon and lampreys, dressed with rich gravies and sweetened with dried fruits. It was a delicacy enjoyed chiefly by the royalty and nobility. Robin Hood sang of pasties in his fourteenth century ballads: "Bred in chese, butre an milk, pastees and flaunes." During this period a French chronicler named Jean Froissart (1337-1414) wrote of men "with botelles of wyne trusses at their sadelles, and pastyes of samonde, troutes, and eyls, wrapped in towels". Today the French call the pasty tourtiere.

The Cornish pasty as we know it was developed some 500 years later. It was filled with beef and potato and usually mixed with slices of onion and swede (or turnip) and seasoning. Curiously, pasties are hardly ever filled with fish, and many Cornish fishermen refuse to take pasties on board when they set out to sea because they believe it will bring them bad luck.

Nobody knows for certain who invented the pasty. There is an old proverb dating back to the middle ages that claims that the Devil would never dare to cross the River Tamar into Cornwall for fear of ending up as pasty filling. This saying probably arose because of the Cornishwomen's propensity to put absolutely anything into their pasties.

From 1150 to 1190 a man called Chretien de Troyes wrote various Arthurian Romances for the Countess of Champagne. One of them, entitled "Eric

Henry VIII's third wife Jane Seymour more than once succumbed to the lure of the Cornish pasty. There is a letter in existence from her baker which states: "hope this pasty reaches you in better condition than the last one".

The humble pasty has even shown up in Shakespeare's plays. Pasties are referenced in *The Merry Wives of Windsor* when Page says: "Wife, bid these gentlemen welcome. Come, we have a hot venison pasty to dinner: come gentlemen, I hope we shall drink down all unkindness." And in *All's Well That Ends Well* Parolles says: "I will confess to what I know without constraint: if ye pinch me like a pasty, I can say no more."

The pasty became a much loved meal for the tin miners of Cornwall. It was practical for the dingy tunnels as the thick pastry crust protected the nourishing ingredients inside. As the miners didn't have time to go above ground for lunch they reheated their pasties on an upturned bucket with a candle burning underneath, or on a shovel held over a head-lamp. The miners' wives stuffed one end of their pasties with meat and vegetables and the other with jam or fruit, so that their husbands could have "two courses". The wives also inscribed the left corner with their husband's initials in order to avoid confusion during lunch (or "croust" as it was known). The Cornish miners often used to leave their personalised corners in offering to the "Knockers", the mischievous elfin creatures who inhabited the mine. The miners believed that the Knockers were responsible for all kinds of misfortune, unless they were given food, in which case they became tokens of good luck.

Over the years the pasty was introduced throughout the country. Variations popped up in Yorkshire, Lancashire and Cumberland, though these may have been brought by Cornish miners who travelled north in search of work. The pasty has since become popular in many areas of the world and May 24th has been declared Pasty Day in the state of Michigan.

Pasties come in various shapes and sizes. In 1985 a group of farmers in Cornwall held the record for making the world's largest pasty. It took seven hours to make, and measured over 32 feet in length. Their record has since been beaten by some bakers in Falmouth who made a giant pasty for the town's first ever Pasty Festival. The pasty has become the greatest Cornish symbol for many people. Whenever the Cornwall rugby team play an important match a huge model pasty is hoisted above the bar before the game begins; the tradition dates back to 1908 and the original pasty is

> "I will confess to what I know without constraint: if ye pinch me like a pasty, I can say no more"

still used to this day.

In 1999 an Anglo-American food war was narrowly avoided when American writer William Grimes deigned to criticise Cornish cuisine in the New York Times: "Cornwall," he said, "probably offers more bad food per square mile than anywhere else in the civilised world... you've got this five pound football-shape thing sitting in your hand and there's nothing you can do with it." The people of Cornwall were incensed by his comments and pasty maker Ann Muller was so angered that she burned an American flag. "I am sorry I burned the flag but Mr Grimes likened the pasty to a door-stop," said Mrs Muller. "The pasty is our emblem," she added. "Its aroma declares we are Cornish." 🌀

THE IDLE COOK

HOT CHOCOLATE & NECK OF LAMB by Alan Porter

HOT CHOCOLATE

Per cup
• 50gms of best dark chocolate. Preferably the Chocolate Society dark organic bar of single estate Madagascan cocoa.
• Some double or whipping cream to top off.
• A dram of your favourite booze or maybe some grond cinnamon,star anise or vanilla extract.
• Lightly whip the cream with the booze or after infusing with the spice.
• Chop the chocolate finelly with a serrated blade.
• Poor on approx 2 tablespoons of boiling water and make a thick mayonnaise (add boiling water a little at a time as necessary) must make smooth emulsion.
• Add more water to taste but approx 125 mls.
• Stir till all chocolate fully dissolved and serve with the cream dolloped on top. Yum.

NECK OF LAMB
WITH PEARL BARLEY

This is one of my favourite simple stews and is very cheap and filling
    You can use lamb breast but it's much fattier. It depends on whether you like lamb fat. I love it.
    Quantities here are a bit up to you but to approx 1kg of neck use 3 cloves garlic, 3 onions, 3 large carrots and a tea cup of barley. To serve three.
• Fry off the meat and veg.

• Add a good sprig of thyme or pinch of parsley stalks, a bay leaf or two if you like it and salt and pepper.
• Pour on boiling water to cover. Bring back to the boil.
• Pour in the barley, put the lid on and stick it in a med to hot oven until it's cooked about 1 and half hours.
• Take the lid off 15 mins before eating to reduce and brown a bit or add more water or a slash of dry white wine.
• Adjust seasoning if necessary and sprinkle with chopped parsley leaf.
I like this stew nice and wet in a bowl with lumps of good brown bread and butter to dunk.
    This is just as good with a cup of teabag tea as with a crisp wine or a pint of beer. ◐

CHLOE KING

CRAP TOWNS

Home of the great Andy Fordham, Dartford is nevertheless a grothole of the highest order

DARTFORD

Population: 86,000 **Unemployment:** 4.2% **Violent Crime (per 1,000 population):** 8.1%
Famous residents: Mick Jagger, Hunter from Gladiators, Andy Fordham

Dartford is only really famous for its tunnel and the 2004 Lakeside Darts Champion Andy Fordham who runs a pub in the town called The Rose. However, according to a startlingly bold statement from the Dartford Town Archive: "A world without Dartford would mean a world without trains, aeroplanes, paper, printing machines, banknotes, tin cans, and miracle medicines." "Delusional mania" should obviously be added to the list.

A glittering tower of east meets west. Yes that's right – all the grimy hopeless industrialisation of east London meets the inbred, horse-farmer mentality of west Kent. The town is entirely circled in a grubby mixture of medium heavy industry and metal fabricators – an industry that might also explain the huge number of people who seem to have some form of physical deformity.

Dartford's amenities include the Saturday market: wall to wall bumbling old codgers, tramps, and teenage mothers swearing at their snotty nosed bawling spawn. Dartford market is also notable for being the only market in England that's actually classier than the shops around it - not that it's good, the rest of the town just seems to be stuck in some kind of post-war rationing hell.

CHRIS JONES ◉

EXILE ON MAIN STREET

STANDING ROOM ONLY

The Connex trains serving Dartford are the worst I've encountered in Britain, in terms of cleanliness, punctuality, service, value for money, politeness of staff and frequency. Generally I stand, usually on something mysteriously sticky and peculiarly human in smell, lest I catch anything from the seats.

CRAP TOWN TRIVIA

Dartford's great son, Mick Jagger, gave a couple of thousand quid to build an arts c entre (desperately needed in a very culturally void area) but the locals complained about the noise, and loud bands are now banned from playing in it.

BETTER THINGS TO DO
THAN READ THIS ADVERT?

THEN THIS IS THE BOOK FOR YOU

CRAP JOBS

Jenny O'Mahony, 17, on her work experience hell

JOURNALIST

My first experience of the working world was a five day stint of work experience at the C___ Times, a local rag based near my school. I entered the building, full of youthful joy and anticipation at having the chance to write for a real paper. I imagined bright, intelligent people, telling me how great this job was, and really, really agreeing as I edited the thoughtful front page I had just completed.

I was directed up some greying, patchy stairs, and entered a mouldy room. A faded picture of Paul Daniels flapped mournfully on the wall, obviously an ill-fated attempt to bring some humour to the desolate landscape of the office. A greying man sat huddled over a computer screen. "I'm the editor," he grunted, staring at me with eyes framed by bags, firmly putting me in my lowly place.

Over the course of the working week, I completed one article about a Naval Association's flag, which was kindly rewritten for me and squashed between two double-glazing adverts on page nine, and a meagre advert for St. Monica's church roof repair fundraiser. Scared stiff by the outbursts of the editor: "Piers Morgan wouldn't know the C___ Times if it shat on his head" (The paper was owned by TrinityMirror) I once sat and stared at a blank computer screen for two hours straight, terrified to ask for anything to do.

Typing was physically difficult, because one journalist, so eager to work he didn't have the time to leave his desk for lunch, had spilt jam from a fat doughnut onto the keyboard, leaving hairy goo in between the f, c and v keys.

People phoned up to settle personal disputes, as in the case of a woman whose son had been kicked in the playground, "for not even any reason" and had had his leg broken. The woman wanted the story published, and the boy who had lashed out to be named and shamed. He was eight. We later found out that the "victim" had in fact taunted the other boy continually, and had just put his middle finger up at him when the attack occurred.

Perhaps the saddest thing I encountered was Helen, a 23 year old who told me: "This job's OK, but I'll get out and start working on something bigger one day." The sick irony of her statement was that she was doomed to work there forever, always on the verge of quitting, but never quite able to hold a gun to the boss's head and get fired, or just ask for a P45.

The day I left, cynical and bitter, one man joked, "Maybe we'll be seeing you again in a few years." I forced out a laugh, whilst thinking how I'd rather eat my own flesh. 🐛

THE IDLE COOK

RICE PUDDING & 4 QUARTERS CAKE by Simon Browne

ARROZ CON LECHE

(RICE PUDDING)

5 quarts water

1 3/4 cups unconverted long-grain white rice

2 quarts scalded milk

3 cups evaporated milk

3 cups sugar, or to taste

2 sticks cinnamon, each about 3 inches long

1/2 cup raisins, or to taste

ground cinnamon to taste for the garnish

Bring 2 quarts water to a boil in a medium saucepan. Remove from heat, and add rice. Let stand for 20 minutes. Rinse rice well, and drain. Bring 3 quarts water to a boil in another saucepan, and add rice. Boil uncovered for 30 minutes or until the rice is tender. (Some rice will take considerably less time). Be careful not to overcook. Drain off excess water.

Mix scalded and evaporated milk, sugar, and cinnamon in a medium saucepan. Cook for 45 minutes or until mixture begins to thicken and changes colour.

Add rice and raisins. Cook for 40 minutes or until pudding thickens. Remove from heat, and stir occasionally until pudding cools thoroughly.

To serve, spoon rice pudding onto a platter, and sprinkle with cinnamon.

The pudding can be cooked until it is very thick, if desired. It also can be shaped into patties and dipped in beaten egg and rolled in bread crumbs before frying in oil and butter until light brown. The patties are rolled in cinnamon and sugar before serving.

Makes 12 servings. From Patricia Quintana's the Taste of Mexico.

FOUR QUARTERS CAKE

A very cheap and easy cake which is also absoutely delicious.

• Take any number of eggs. Even one egg will do.

• Weigh them/it.

• Take the same weight of butter, flour and sugar.

• Break the egg into a bowl and beat the lot together with your chosen flavour, eg lemon zest, or good vanilla essence.

• Pour into a buttered and floured cake tin.

• Bake at 180 for about half an hour or until a knife slides through the cake without sticking.

• Turn out and serve with crème fraiche and raspberries. ➲

Neville by Tony Husband

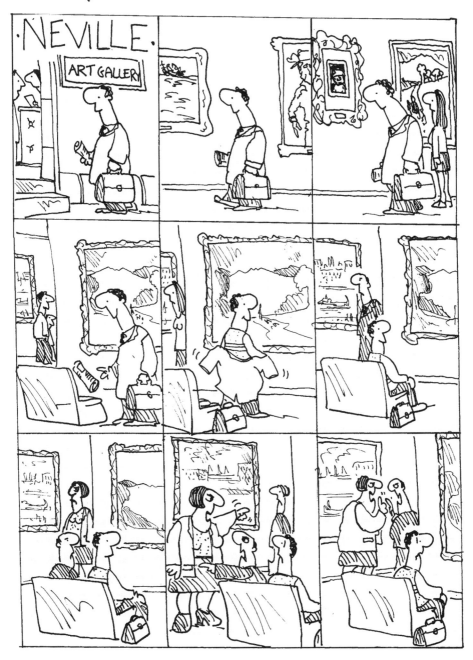

THE IDLER QUESTIONNAIRE:
RICHARD MABEY

is the naturalist and author of the classic foraging book, *Food For Free*. He is also the biographer of TH White. He lives on a farm in Norfolk.

What time do you get up?
Sometimes 6pm in spring, sometimes 9.30 in deep winter.

Do you leap up or lie slumbering?
Not so much slumbering, more smouldering.

Do you smoke and drink, and if so, how much?
Don't smoke. Drink wine in moderation, but with relish.

How many hours work do you put in on an average day?
Maybe nine hours when on a book. But of course being my own boss, I can put in 80 hour weeks when I need to, and then take a week off at an hour's notice.

Do you take holidays?
Yes, but they never turn into "absences from work". I've tried to do that, and go lala in a few days.

Where do you live?
In Roydon, in the Upper Waveney Valley in Norfolk.

Where do you work?
Ditto, in an annex to our farmhouse which has come to be called the Scriptorum.

Where do you think?
Anywhere. Trains are brilliant, something to do with having no responsibilities, I suspect.

What are your three greatest pleasures?
The thrill of an idea taking shape, or a piece of work well done. Fabulous birds en fete (plenty up in Norfolk, including cranes). Dancing with Poppy.

Do you like money?
Yes, but only to use.

Are you happy?
Content. Being uncomplicatedly happy has always seemed to me a sign of gross insensitivity!

How many hours do you sleep at night/day?
Six at night if lucky. Have never got on with sleep.

What are you reading?
Ronald Blythe's astonishing historical novel, The Assassin, and, for work, Robert Elliot's Faking Nature, and Claude Levi-Strauss, Honey to Ashes..

If it came to the crunch, would you choose money or art?
Forging. Like Vulcan, I mean.

What have you been thinking about?
Onset of winter. Being ill. I'm an unreconstructed hypochondriac.

Who are your heroes?
John Clare, Bob Dylan, Annie Dillard, Edward Abbey...

USEFUL FOR THE CASH POOR, TIME RICH

Any advice for young people?
Being old is the best time to spend being young.

Do you like to go a-wandering?
Never do much else. But round the interior of the hourse, very slowly, on all fours, can be as exciting as the Matto Grosso.

What is paradise?
South of France, late May. Cistus in bloom. Nightingales, bee-eaters, and a bottle of Mas de Daumas. ◉

BILL & ZED'S BAD ADVICE

WE'VE FUCKED UP OUR LIVES. NOW IT'S YOUR TURN

Zen Master Zed could not be contacted for this issue as he is in New Orleans drinking whisky sours and shooting crocodiles. So this time, you've got unadorned Bill

Dear Zen Masters,
It's all very well telling us to be idlers, but how do you afford it?
Peeved and Confused, New Malden

Dear Peeved and Confused,
The whole Idler thing is a front for some of the most career scrabbling, hard working, Oxbridge educated nonces in our modern world. This is how it works: they promote idleness as a lifestyle option, you buy into it because it sounds cool; you buy the books, the events, the TV shows even the t-shirts, and they make the money.The people who actually print the books in China and make the t-shirts in India work all the hours and get paid a pittance.
So what you've got to do is come up with your own concept of a seductive lifestyle option that you can con people to buy into and exploit it to the max. Thus you make lots of money and then you can be as idle as you want.

Dear Zen Masters,
I believe the guitar to be the principal tool of youthful rebellion. Would you agree?
Johnny B, Hackney

Dear B Boring,
How fuckin' wrong can you be? The guitar, especially the electric variety, has been the Soma handed out to teenage lads of a slightly questioning nature for the last

fifty years. That is since your grandfather bought Bill Haley's "Rock Around The Clock" and your dad bought Never Mind The Bollocks and you bought the White Stripes. They buy the electric guitar thinking they are going to change the world with it. The only thing that changes is that they trade in their ideals for vain dreams of rock stardom, which at some point, however successful they become, withers and dies to be replaced by a festering bitterness.
Which country in the world invented the electric guitar? Which country has more electric guitars per head of population? Which country in the world has been able to turn teenage rebellion into just another consumer choice for the rest of the world to buy into and for them to reap the fiscal rewards? Which country in the world is the most politically and religiously reactionary?
Forget railing against Coca Cola and McDonald's, get over to Norwich and get the can of kerosene and box of Swan Vesta before that loser Libertines fan and burn down the nearest shop selling electric guitars.

Dear Zen Masters,
I am soon to be a dad for the first time and I am petrified. How will I manage to maintain an active social life?
Kevin, Forest Gate

BAD ADVICE CONTINUED

Dear Kevin,

I've never been one for the active social life. Never been one for bonhomie of any sort, that said Z and myself have sired between us at least nine children from six assorted females. Not once has any of these births stopped us doing what ever the fuck we wanted.

Of course there is nothing to stop any of these offspring we have littered the world with come looking for us with a shot gun and a list of demands.

Dear Zen Masters,

I am 17 and I can clearly see for myself how the wage system is designed to enslave the majority for the benefit of the few. But my parents keep on at me to get a job. What can I say to them to get them off my back?
Libertines fan, Norwich

Dear Libertines fan,

First you are wrong, no one is a wage slave. We are all free to do what the fuck we want and walk away from whatever responsibilities we may think we have. Of course you might not be able to handle that freedom or take the shit that comes with it. As for your mum and dad, you are obviously one of those young men that I keep hearing about, who want to be mollycoddled in the family home, where everything is provided, for as long as possible, so you don't have to think about council tax, TV licences and water rates. And why the fuck should you if you don't want to? So my suggestion to you is: take an axe to the umbilical cord that is obviously holding you back from achieving your true potential. Next, get the can of

kerosene and box of Swan Vesta that I will leave outside Anglia TV Centre in Norwich at 3pm on 17 December 2004; return to the family home and burn the place down with whatever remains of your mum and dad inside. Walk away from the place taking nothing with you, not even your name. Your life will never be the same again and the adventure will have only just begun...

Shit! I have just reread your letter and remembered that you're a Libertines fan. Forget everything I have said above. The Libertines are such a retro band and anybody that is a fan of them is obviously just into getting their kicks vicariously, wanting somebody else to live the life of a would be bohemian, crack cocaine addicted poet for them, while there is always Mothers Pride in the bread bin for that slice of toast and marmite however late you get up for breakfast.

Get a fuckin' job.

Dear Zen Masters,

The TV licence bastards are making my life a misery. They keep calling me and hassling me. Their letters get heavier and heavier. I gave all my details on the phone but they are still hassling me. Any advice?
Frieda, Notting Hill

Dear Frieda,

Serves you fuckin' right for watching TV in the first place. TV exists to serve the same ends as the electric guitar (see above). While you are watching TV, you are doing fuck all with your time to fulfil your potential and ultimately make the world a better place.

Throw your TV out the window. Get

over to Norwich and get that can of Kerosene and box of Swan Vesta, because that arsehole, that obviously is not not going to grow out of his infatuation with the electric guitar, won't, and burn down the nearest Curry's.

Dear Zen Masters,

The VISA people keep raising my limit without me asking, forcing me to spend more money. They make it difficult to cancel it. I am getting into worse and worse debt.
Frieda, Notting Hill

Dear Frieda again,

What the fuck is wrong with the people who read this column. I thought you readers of the Idler were individuals that had taken control of your lives, knew how the world worked. It seems to me that you are just buying it in the hope that you are buying into some vaguely hip, London centric scene, that's all about hanging out with some vaguely famous people who do fuck all but make you feel you are a loser because you are not one of them.

Debt is just a fiction. You can't wear it, eat it or sleep with it. Debt was made up by the modern equivalent of those that made up the concept of Satan, to keep people in their place.

Plastic money started with American Express, I rest my case.

Dear Zen Masters,

I am trying to give up smoking. I didn't have the mental capability to resist the advertising when I was younger, and now all this money goes on smoking ... it upsets me that I am addicted... I am trappped. There is no way out. What can I do?
Frieda, Notting Hill

Dear Frieda,

Are your orgasms as multiple as your problems?

I know that it has been popular with what ever sub-socia economical strata in society I inhabit, for as long as I can remember to blame the United States of America for all the ills of the world, but for fuck's sake, where had Raleigh been when he first brought back tobacco to these shores? Even if he got the stuff off what you might think of as the noble savage, it was still America.

Look, I know you, the Libertine fan, or Johnny B Boring will not get off your arses to get over to Anglia TV Centre in Norwich and get the can of Kerosene and box of Swan Vesta. It will just be removed by a traffic warden of the commissioner for Anglia TV. So instead of wasting it, I will send them by courier to the first person who writes to me via the Idler who promises me they will use them to burn down a guitar shop, a TV shop or a shop selling cigarettes.

The revolution starts today. ☺

CONVERSATIONS

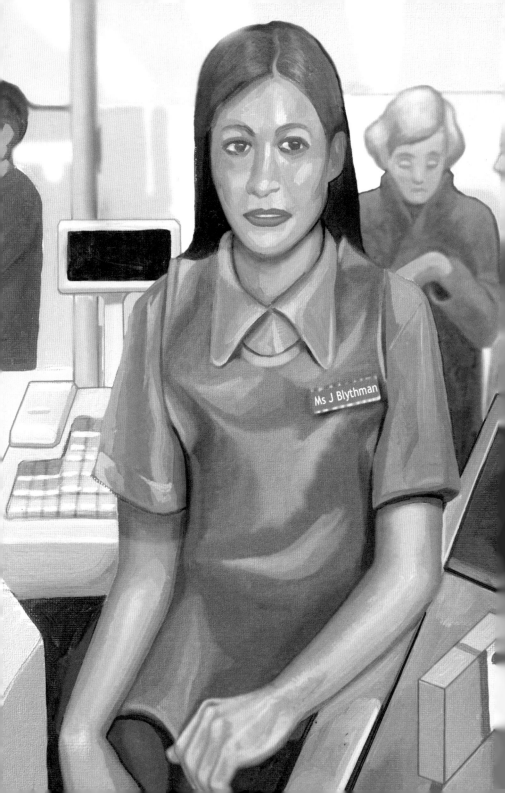

IN CONVERSATION WITH

JOANNA BLYTHMAN

Dan Kieran went to meet the renowned author of *Shopped: The Shocking Power of British Supermarkets.*
Illustration by Jeff Harrison

We love supermarkets. We must do because eighty percent of the food we eat in Britain comes from them. Supermarkets have made food cheaper than it used to be, we have more choice today than before they were here and they've made shopping much more convenient. Or have they? Not according to Joanna Blythman.

IDLER: We loved your book, it is very *Idler*-ish in the sense that it tells the truth. But reading it was terrifying. Did the things you found out shock you?
BLYTHMAN: I thought I was going to find problems with the way the supermarkets operated and I went through a phase of being shocked. One farmer who had literally to chip leeks out of a frozen field on his hands and knees with a chisel to prevent his company losing its supermarket contract. I remember going back to the car thinking, "Oh my God, it's so awful!" But then I just became used to the horror of it, so now I take it for granted that supermarkets behave in this way.

The suppliers are so feudal. I'm not very business minded, but when they say to you they're growing hundreds of acres of vegetables for a supermarket but they don't have a contract... I thought, doesn't every business rely on contracts? I just didn't know anything about it. But that's when you start to realise where the power lies.

IDLER: You say that ready meals have had a huge impact on whether people buy raw ingredients.

BLYTHMAN: That is the most worrying thing. When the older generation is gone there will be almost no one alive other than butchers who know what a properly hung piece of beef looks like. It's like a chain of knowledge that's being eroded because of the way supermarkets have changed how we eat.

IDLER: My Gran says, "You don't realize how many different varieties of apples there are."

BLYTHMAN: Supposedly supermarkets give us this fabulous choice and before

supermarkets we were in this state of rationing, you know, black and white films. It's quite a psychological achievement when you look at how narrow the choice really is. There is a choice, but it's not a qualitative choice. The real variety, the different crops that we used to grow have all gone. Very few people have challenged the supermarket idea that they provide choice.

IDLER: The other thing that supermarkets have managed to persuade us is that they're cheap,

BLYTHMAN: And that's another myth. I bought cherries from my local greengrocer the other day, and they were £4.75 a kilo so I bought two kilos, fantastic cherries, but in Marks and Spencers down the road they were £8 a kilo. The mark-up is staggering on fruit and vegetables.

IDLER: How do they get away with it?

BLYTHMAN: I think we just don't challenge it, we don't have time. But also it's quite cunning. Supermarkets sell cherries, for example, in 350 gram packs and they seem bigger than they are. When you get them home and you take the lid off you can't believe how few cherries are actually in there. But they'll have a few things, like bananas, which will be really cheap to help create the idea that everything else is. Unless you buy the really

TROLLEY TOWNS

From *Shopped: The Shocking Power of British Supermarkets* (4th Estate, £12.99)

The term "company town" was coined by historians to describe centres of population made distinctive by the one-dimensional nature of their employment opportunities and the predominance of the large companies that controlled them. Nowadays it may be more apt to distinguish places not according to how locals earn their money, but by how they spend it. Few British towns have a distinctive sense of place any longer. Most have become trolley towns, shaped by

heavily processed foods, things like baked beans, you'll find that supermarkets are actually much more expensive than small shops and markets.

IDLER: I get my shopping from Sainsbury's every week. I want to go to markets but I never seem to have the time. I live quite near Borough Market and I go there sometimes but that always seems to be really expensive.

BLYTHMAN: London's different from other places because you don't have such huge supermarkets, at least not in the centre anyway. If you go somewhere like Hull you'll find that they dominate the town.

IDLER: When we were working on *Crap Towns* we'd get sent emails from people saying, "these supermarkets come in, it decimates the town centre, it rips the heart out of the community," but in their adverts the supermarkets try and give the impression that they're part of the community.

BLYTHMAN: It's really disingenuous. In medieval times the centre of civilisation, the big populated areas, was the cathedral and now it's the shopping centre. And have you noticed how they always have very pretentious architecture?

IDLER: I went on a road trip after *Crap Towns* came out and visited a place called South Woodham Ferrers which is essentially Asdatown. The weird thing was that the town itself was empty, there wasn't a soul around. But I went into the ASDA and it was packed!

BLYTHMAN: Because there's nothing else to do. Going back to farmers markets, I think Borough market, from what I hear, is a bit self-consciously "cool".

IDLER: Yeah, it's a bit like that.

BLYTHMAN: I go to Scottish farmers' markets and they're not like that at all. You tend to get the slightly hippyish hill-walking vegan who's about ninety but looks sixty. But then you get lots of parents with young children, who are obviously put off by the supermarkets' lack of quality and high prices. Farmers' markets are actually quite cheap. There are waiting lists for people who want stalls at some farmers markets, some of them are turning over

the grocery chains that dominate them.

What does a trolley town look like? Approach any significant centre of population in the UK and you must pass through the supermarket ring. The first thing that greets you is not some distinctive civic monument or landmark but the now familiar supermarket sprawl, complete with its new roundabouts, altered road layout, traffic signals with changed priorities, petrol station and sea of parking. Welcome to Asdatown, or Tescotown, or Sainsburytown. Make it into the centre of one of these places and you're in Anytown, Anywhere. Or even Clonetown. You'll search to find anything approximating to a small greengrocer,

fishmonger or butcher. These have been replaced by charity shops, video shops and, in more affluent centres, branches of large retail chains. This is the new urban landscape our large supermarket chains have bequeathed us.

Dundee is a typical trolley town, or city. Once an important port at the mouth of the River Tay, its heyday was during the industrial revolution. Dundee's reputation was built on the three Js: jam, jute and journalism. By dint of its seafaring history, Dundee claims the credit for introducing Britain to the delights of jam made from imported exotic fruits, otherwise known as marmalade. In the nineteenth century, its jute mills swelled

ten grand in a Saturday morning, it works really well. I don't think enough people realise that farmers' markets are a realistic alternative to supermarket shopping.

IDLER: It's only a matter of time before the supermarkets catch up though.

BLYTHMAN: Well some of them have tried to have them in their car parks. It's all part of this move to show that they're not against farmers' markets.

IDLER: The other thing is that supermarkets make great claims about the quality of the food they sell but people are more and more afraid of what they're eating. You tell the story of the chicken that had been condemned, so a supplier pumped it full of chemicals, bleached the skin to make it look white and then dumped it...

BLYTHMAN: Yes, it turned up in a ready meal in Waitrose...

IDLER: I would never eat a ready meal now. I used to. I used to think of them as being a treat! You know: I've worked hard, I'm worn out, I deserve a night off cooking, so I'll spend four quid on this thing.

BLYTHMAN: I remember as a child there was a thing called Vesta chicken curry, and I pleaded with my mother to buy me one and she refused, saying they were terrible and so on. I remember on the adverts they had really exotic looking women, belly dancing. And one night when my parents were going out she asked me what I wanted for dinner and I said Vesta chicken curry, so she said alright then, go on I'll buy you one. And I was so excited but of course the reality was a kind of slop on a plastic tray. I had the most acute sense of disappointment and I think I've never got over that in many ways. I have ready meals every now and then and every time I end up thinking: Oh gosh, I would've been better off eating bread and cheese. On a gastronomic level it's appalling. It's been cooked three times, it's got modified starch and caramel colouring, but forget all that, it's just the fact that it's such a miserable thing to eat. I guess what's worrying though is that people's point of

TROLLEY TOWNS CONTINUED...

its population. In the twentieth century, it was better known as the home of the *Beano* and the *Dandy* comics created by local publisher D.C. Thomson. Now Dundee has a population of around 165,000. On paper, it is an interesting place to live in and visit, and not short of visual attractions. It has the silvery Tay itself and the Tay Rail Bridge, a dark mass of sturdy Victorian metal. You can still see the stump of its notorious predecessor, the one that collapsed into the river. You can visit the historic sailing ship the *Discovery*, famed for its early exploration of the Arctic. But the first thing that hits

you when you approach Dundee from any direction these days is not this unique and impressive heritage but supermarkets.

In the 1990s Dundee was home to William Low, a Scottish supermarket chain with relatively small stores throughout the country. It was acquired by Tesco as a quick way for it to build its base in Scotland and compete with the then dominant chain, Safeway. Soon the whole look of Dundee started to change. Locals were amazed when, after the council had spent lots of money improving the approaches to the city, planting floral displays, landscaping and so on, Tesco got planning permission for a superstore on

reference is "Oh Waitrose lasagne! That's good. That's a nice Friday night in." It makes you aware and you start to think where's our culinary culture going? You wouldn't catch the French or the Italians eating something like that.

IDLER: But we watch all these cookery programmes, we buy thousands of cookery books, is it just porn food?

BLYTHMAN: It's gastro-porn and it's also virtual food reality where we watch more and more food on the TV and these programmes are supposed to be consumed while we're sitting in front of the telly eating a ready meal. There's no evidence that cookery programmes are making people cook more. People are clearly cooking less, the average cooking time for an evening meal is twenty minutes and people think that's going to go down to ten quite soon. If you look at the enormous amount of cookery books and the cookery book industry then there's obviously some disjunction. It doesn't quite add up. But again it's another example of the food business. We think we're interested in food but we shop exclusively in supermarkets, it's just another part of not doing food very well in this country.

I think we're even more dependent on

We think we're interested in food but we shop exclusively in supermarkets

supermarkets than in America. I've been speaking to people who are saying that even Americans can't stomach supermarket food. Of course you've got the enormous places like Wal-Mart but there are more and more independent food outlets. It's a really British thing, that addiction to supermarkets. It's just another piece of evidence to argue that we really don't understand food very well. Otherwise we wouldn't allow the

the city's most desirable and scenic location, Riverside Drive, with its long, open views over the river Tay. Then Asda started flexing its muscles and Sainsbury's entered the fray. Now most key routes through and past Dundee seem to lead to vast supermarkets. They loom so large that they dwarf the city's outstanding historic and civic heritage. The city struggles to put itself on the tourist map, and no wonder: to the visitor, it might look as though the main occupation of its residents is supermarket shopping.

Dundee city centre consists of an area of about half a square mile, large parts of which are pedestrianised. At either end,

like sentinels, stand two shopping malls, tenanted with a familiar litany of chain shops - Carphone Warehouse, Claire's Accessories, Clinton Cards and so on. Fast-food chains are also well represented. Most of the small shop units that remain in the centre have been turned into pubs or amusement centres, or charity or video rental shops.

In the 1960s, before the large UK-wide supermarket chains managed to persuade Dundee's impoverished city council, desperate for cash, to let them have their way, this area was a thriving centre for food shopping. There were ten bakers; now there are two left. There were eight or nine butchers; now there is

supermarkets to provide us with all of our food despite how they promote themselves. I mean their agenda is not good food. IDLER: Do you think there's much hope for the future? BLYTHMAN: I think there is. I use the analogy that it's like being in a bad relationship for a long time, you know, you suddenly wake up one morning and you look at the person and you think, 'I've been with you for ages and actually I've realized this morning that I really hate you. I'm now re-running all the things that I thought I liked about you over in my mind and I've realised I actually hate them and they really get on my nerves' and I think people are beginning to feel this way about supermarkets, they're beginning to realize that there is an alternative. I think it's on the edge and it can change. Particularly the way these enormous supermarkets just keep getting built, people are beginning to feel, "Oh my God, not another Tesco" which is the way it's going. Every petrol station is run by Tesco, their local convenience store is run by Sainsbury. I don't think that British consumers are up for that, even if they don't care about food, or they don't know about food very much. I mean you must have come across this in *Crap Towns*, people care very much about the High Street, their locality, and their town not being exactly the same as every other town, it's so alienating being in a place which is just the same as every other place with a Sainsbury's.

IDLER: We got hundreds of emails from people complaining that every town in Britain looks identical, every town could be called crap.

BLYTHMAN: I think that is something British people can get quite militant about. That might be the thing that will make people put their foot down more than anything else. People will identify supermarkets as being a huge part of that problem. But what I'm trying to do with the book is say: Yes, supermarkets have enormous power and they are doing terrible things to our food and the way we eat. But a lot of people can't see how that is going to change. It's going to get much worse. I'm trying

TROLLEY TOWNS CONTINUED...

one. Of the five fishmongers, one has survived. Where there were half a dozen grocers, one remains. Food shoppers – as opposed to food grazers – will find little to sustain them in Dundee city centre these days.

When I visited Dundee in 2003, the city had four Tescos, two Safeways, two Asdas, one Sainsbury's, one Marks & Spencer and a clutch of discount and low-price outlets. Asda had submitted a planning application to build a third store on a greenfield site. It had commissioned a traffic-impact study to support its application and was reported to be 'ready and waiting' to state its case to councillors when it came before the planning committee. Residents, meanwhile, had formed an action group to oppose the application. Not to be left out of Dundee's supermarket mêlée, Morrisons was also in talks with the city council over its application to build a further 90,000-square-foot superstore in the city, close in scale to a Tesco Extra or an Asda superstore. Since both the Asda and Morrisons proposed sites were on council land, Dundee City Council stood to receive a substantial windfall from the sales. 'Some estimates have put the amount the local authority stands to make at anywhere between £15 and £20

to say to people, do you realise that? Are you up for that? Are you happy to let that happen? And I think that's where we are with this book, you have to say to people: 'We're not going to get rid of them, but we can stop them being in control of everything we eat.' That's why we have to challenge the perception people have of supermarkets. One of the things I've tried to challenge is the idea that supermarkets are so convenient, I don't see what's so convenient about getting in your car and driving miles every time you want a carton of milk. What happened to the doorstep pint of milk? I get a box of fruit and veg delivered every week, it tastes great, it's convenient and it's better value that the supermarket.

IDLER: Maybe that's the answer, you've got to prove to people that there is an alternative.

BLYTHMAN: But we've got to encourage the people that are hanging on, the independent shops, the butchers and bakers. We have to say "we are committed to you, we are going to make a point of supporting shops like yours". Because we're at a tipping point now, it may seem as though supermarkets have it all but there's still 20% of the market that they want. Thankfully we've got a lot of Asian shops with alternative, fantastic produce who make a tremendous contribution to the independent sector. But if people could transfer just 5% of their total shopping budget to greengrocers, butchers and bakers it would make an enormous difference. We have to send the people that are still here a very clear message, "hang around because we want you, we value you". Even if you only change small things, like don't buy your newspaper from a supermarket, get it delivered. Every time you buy a bottle of wine don't buy it from a supermarket, get it from the off license. Even shops like Oddbins and Threshers are petrified of supermarkets now. But if we don't support these shops they *will* vanish and then we won't have a choice about where we buy our food. And in whose interest is that? ⌨

million,' reported the *Evening Telegraph*. Dundee clearly did not need any more supermarkets. Yet with this sort of money to play for, you could see why councillors might be sorely tempted to say yes to a couple more...

It is a familiar story, one that can be recounted time and time again by people living in every part of the UK. When the big supermarkets move in, towns and cities are pushed to what the New Economics Foundation calls the "tipping point". When the number of local retail outlets falls below a critical mass, the quantity of money circulating in the local economy suddenly plummets as people find there is no point in trying to do a full shop where the range of local outlets is impoverished. "This means a sudden, dramatic loss of services – leading to food and finance deserts," says the Foundation. In the case of big centres of population, this desertification expresses itself in a carbon-copy townscape dominated by omnipresent chains and fast-food outlets. In small places, it manifests itself in one of two forms: either pretty, but useless, main streets with a dearth of everyday services, or wholesale depression and deadness. ⌨

FEATURES

ON NOT HAVING A CAREER

Joan Bakewell explains why she never wanted a proper job. Illustrations by Anthony Haythornthwaite

"And what would you like to be when you grow up?" I asked my five-year old grand-daughter. Blythly she came back with a show-stopper of an answer: "A butterfly," she said with all the serious intent of her years. We have to take such aspirations calmly. They indicate a wish for a colourful life, wafted gently on summer breezes from fragrant flower to fragrant flower, preferably somewhere within a golden expanse of English countryside. You could do worse. Indeed, apart from certain problems concerning species, her vision of the future has the essence of an idyll many of us would recognize. So how come we're caught on the 8.10am to Euston most mornings, or locked in a traffic jam on the M62? We're having a career, that's the reason. And we never reckoned it would involve so much unpleasantness.

I come from a generation many of whom didn't give much thought to a career until we were well into our third year at university. Those were the days of education for its own sake, and being a student was to be enjoyed simply for itself. Some were training to be architects and doctors, but many of those taking humanities courses allowed things to drift. There had been no career advice at school, and no thought taken for the morrow. (The church still had a strong hold and such Christian aphorisms still clung.) That's how I came to have a shot at a series of jobs that might, had I persisted, have made me a Charles Saatchi, or a Heather Brigstock, the former and formidable High Mistress of St Paul's Girls' School.

But first I had had an epiphany moment. In the mid-Fifties I travelled regularly on the underground into central London to a BBC job at which I was not very good. If you're no good at something, you're not happy and I was looking for change.

Suddenly it struck me. Carriages of people crammed together, sweaty body to sweaty body. Stern of countenance, sour of demeanour, day after day. I totted up what a lifetime of such journeys might mean if I stayed with such a routine. It was far too much time. I wanted to spend every moment enjoying life to the full, not enduring such discomfort for the time-being in the hope of pleasures to come. I had recently seen Fritz Lang's film *Metropolis*, and I pictured myself all too clearly as one of its anonymous figures, faceless and characterless, plodding their

> **I decided there and then that I would deliberately seek work whose routine did not conform to the daily grind**

way through an urban nightmare. I decided then and there I would deliberately seek work whose routine did not conform to the daily grind.

I tried teaching. There are many things to commend teaching. A post can usually be found close to home, which means walking or cycling to work. The hours differ from that of office slaves, the work is personal and engaging, caught up in human relationships and children's development. It had all this going for it. Unhappily, there was not much going for me. I was no good. I couldn't keep order, I was terrorised by the children. Only briefly did I enjoy that magical moment when I caught their attention and held it, and we both enjoyed what we were

learning together. But the strain was too great. I lacked the presence and the strength to see it through. Being unhappy, I gave up.

I gave advertising a good shot. I became a copywriter and quite enjoyed it. This, regrettably, did involve the dreaded routine journey to work. But I made the best of it. I took a bus from the Hampstead terminal, cornered a window seat at the front and read my way to work. Once there, I enjoyed the upbeat and witty company of lively people conspiring to create clever advertising campaigns together. This can be exhilarating. We had fun and success. And perhaps if I'd stuck with it I could by now be a millionaire advertising guru with a gallery full of modern pictures to prove it. But no. Wouldn't I have to climb the ladder, become top dog, sweet-talk banks, set up companies, employ and – worse – sack others? No thanks. Sounds too much like a career for me.

By now I was beginning to formulate what exactly I wanted from life. Not from a job or even a career. But from life itself. And I discovered that the ingredients actually lay all around. They just needed to be combined in the right formula to meet my own temperament and abilities. They are not obscure and elusive. They are the very things most of us want: a happy family life focused around good relationships; congenial surroundings both at home and at work, that make life pleasant. I am not talking some ambitious make-over nonsense here. Think instead of being able to watch a particular tree round the seasons, coming into bud,

Think of being able to watch a particular tree round the seasons, coming into bud, flowering, turning to golden leaf... that seems to be a good ambition to have

flowering, turning to golden leaf and then fronting the winter with stark, dramatic branches. That seems to be a good ambition to have. Then there are friendships; bosom pals for intimacies and advice; working colleagues for sustaining each other with laughter and encouragement; acquaintances met at odd moments, introduced by others, casually encountered at the school gate. All these friendships settle and regroup over the years, some coming to the fore, others lapsing with time. Yes, the encouragement of friendship seems a worthwhile way of spending time. Finally there is the work itself. My own needs are for variety of tasks within and possibly at the limit of my capabilities, periods of heavy effort

interspersed with more reflective times; intellectual engagement with ideas, and a sense of something worthwhile being achieved.

I was to find a way of life that combined all these criteria. What would have tipped the whole thing out of balance would have been having a high-powered career. What happened was this. I had noticed in my first unhappy foray into the BBC that there were people called broadcasters who came and went at odd hours, undertook either major creative enterprises, radio drama, for example, or modest, brief talks, say, on *Woman's Hour*. Each of them had creative freedom, the collaboration of amiable staff, and went away with a cheque. It's called being a freelance. It was the life for me.

I made my way slowly, and always have. Once it became clear to enough people that I could handle an interview, there were numerous opportunities. I travelled the country to make the most of them, because in those days ITV consisted of some twelve companies. I've worked in my day for Granada, for Anglia, for ATV, for Westward, for Harlech and for Southern. It was at the latter, on a regular afternoon programme for women called "Home at 4.30" that I really cut my teeth. We recorded three programmes on a single day: quick turnaround, lively ideas, interviews you researched and planned for yourself. Yes, this combined all the criteria I had so consciously enumerated for myself. And as a bonus the return journey to London involved afternoon cream teas in the cushioned and wood-panelled Pullman

I have never become a producer, director, a manager of any sort. I have thus avoided responsibility, worry, ambition, jealousy and back-biting

that was once the glory of the railways.

I had found what I enjoyed doing. Making television programmes. And I was to go on doing it. For over thirty years I have enjoyed as much variety and interest as I longed for. I have never become a producer, a director, a manager of any sort. I have thus avoided responsibility, worry, ambition, jealousy and back-biting. I have also avoided promotion, grand titles and the higher executive earnings. I have turned down what I didn't fancy, and accepted with wholehearted commitment what I enjoy. I have simply gone on doing the same thing, and I still do. Not having a career has been a great career choice. ☻

PLEASURE PRINCIPLES

Orlando Radice meets Carlo Petrini, founder of the radical and humane Slow Food movement

Back in the 1980s, while Margaret Thatcher was deregulating our asses, opening us up to foreign markets and whipping the economy into a frenzy of white-collar capitalism, the Italians were getting their first taste of Big Macronomics.

While we got the full meal deal of more homogenising food chains, a flexible labour market and pulverised trade unions, Italy just got a retail makeover – over 1700 new supermarkets appeared in 1980-89.

But down on that sun-blessed peninsular there were still plenty of slow, community-based, small-scale producers of quality food working at a nice leisurely pace. Sustainable idling, if you will – and it looked like its days were numbered.

So when McDonald's tried to set up by the Spanish Steps in 1986, a group of Italian activists, led by Carlo Petrini, went to Rome to demonstrate. They didn't stop McDonald's from opening, but they did go to Paris three years later to agree on a manifesto that established the Slow Food movement. They promised to resist the "universal madness of 'the fast life'" with tranquil material pleasure" by teaching people to enjoy the full biodiversity of the world's food products. This, they argued, would be the perfect way to fend off culturally invasive forms of global trade and its accompanying low-grade fuel: fast food.

Quite a mission, but fast forward to 2004 and Slow Food has become an alternative universe. It has a large publishing arm, a

> "The pleasure that we are reclaiming and defending is the expression of an aware and guided hedonism, not an end in itself."

> "In an evolved society, quality should be the right of everybody, not just a few, and I say that notwithstanding those who believe that our movement is snobbish."

> "The father of slowness is Seneca, the Spanish philosopher who maintained that life is not short but we burn it up too fast."

PIZZA AND WINE: THE ITALIANS HAVE GOT THEIR PRIORITIES STRAIGHT

university, a group in Brussels lobbying the EU on agriculture policy, links to TV channels and more than 80,000 members in all five continents with branches in 50 countries.

In Britain, the Slow Food revolution arrived in 1998. Unfortunately by that time many of our traditional cheese, sausage and beer producers were either gone or in difficulty (although a few revived), and today the UK arm of movement has a little above 1000 members. Despite our battery of effective pressure groups, people who wanted to do good have traditionally stuck to animals, human rights and ecosystems, and everyone worthy – with the mild exception of CAMRA (Campaign For Real Ale) – gave cultural politics a wide bypass.

Perhaps that's why some UK commentators have had trouble appreciating the full flavour of the Slow Food movement. It is neither simply an unaligned pressure group, defined mechanically by what it opposes – à la Amnesty – nor an élite group of gastronomes who don't worry about whether or not people can afford their way of life. Instead, Slow Food has created a complete, politicised counter culture with plenty of grassroots support.

Of course, Slow Food opposes fast food and large-scale agribusiness – but it mainly wants to prove that the slow production of quality food, its sociable consumption and the preservation of local products, is a realistic mass-goal for society. And it argues that with the help of education, all this can grow out of a nation's traditions.

On the charge of élitism, Petrini admits that non-industrial nosh will cost more, but argues that if we spent less on things like cars and more

Socialist thinking is, in fact, in the blood for Slow Foodies

on taste then even people who consider themselves poor could afford it. What's more, the pleasure of eating in company is fundamentally levelling because, he says, "pleasure is a way of being at one with yourself and others."

Socialist thinking, in fact, is in the blood for Slow Foodies. Petrini started out as a journalist for left-wing Italian papers like *L'Unità*, and his inspiration for Slow Food partly came from the popularity of Gambero Rosso, in the 1980s a pro-slow gastronomic supplement of the leftish national *Il Manifesto*.

The material source for the movement was Arcigola, a national food and wine association that Petrini co-founded and then converted into Slow Food. Arcigola in turn had been an offshoot of Arci (Associazione Ricreativa Culturale Italiana), a network of social clubs – supported by the Italian Communist Party – that gives communities the locations

"Slow Food means giving the act of nutrition its appropriate value, learning to enjoy the full variety of recipes and flavours available, acknowledging the diversity of producers and their localities, respecting the rhythms of the seasons and of living together."

"Advice for British consumers? I would advise them to pay attention to biological, environment-friendly agriculture, and to start valuing it. And so would like to see the dissemination of more information on this matter in the UK, and following from this, a renaissance in British agriculture."

PETRINI SUDDENLY RECALLS A FINE PIEDMONT CHEESE

and funding to eat, drink, dance and have a good time.

"From the left we learnt and created our tradition of solidarity and mutuality," says Petrini. But it was from the radical US politician Ralph Nader that Petrini got his first lesson in setting up a self-sufficient cultural organisation. "Arci had huge debts at the time and when Ralph Nader saw our membership

"We have no enemies. There is no conflict with other worlds, we operate through dialogue. We would not like to dis-solve diff-erent visions of the world."

of around 1.5 million, he encouraged me to use business tactics with Arcigola. I saw that it was important to be both economically solid and independent."

Slow Food didn't become overtly political until 1990, when Petrini and the Slow Food promotions manager Roberto Burdese helped organise the electoral campaign for a Radical Party candidate in the Piedmont regional elections (Slow Food's constituency). "It was a disaster," says Burdese, and the Democrazia Cristiana wiped out all other parties. Good came of it, though. Slow Food switched from representational to grass roots politics, and by 1995 they had 20,000 members.

In 1995 the organisation broadened its campaigning remit to protect the diversity of

"We proudly reclaim the value of gastronomic sciences and the knowledge (or really the idea of knowledge and wisdom united) that has been passed down from generation to generation. Connecting this knowledge with the defence of the environment, sustainability and the defence of biodiversity is what makes us who we are and different to other environment movements."

SLOW FOOD MANIFESTO

INTERNATIONAL MOVEMENT FOR THE DEFENCE OF AND THE RIGHT TO PLEASURE ...

Born and nurtured under the sign of Industrialization, this century first invented the machine and then modelled its lifestyle after it. Speed became our shackles. We fell prey to the same virus: "the fast life" that fractures our customs and assails us even in our own homes, forcing us to ingest "fast-food".

Homo sapiens must regain wisdom and liberate itself from the "velocity" that is propelling it on the road to extinction. Let us defend ourselves against the universal madness of "the fast life" with tranquil material pleasure.

Against those – or, rather, the vast majority – who confuse efficiency with frenzy, we propose the vaccine of an adequate portion of sensual gourmandise pleasures, to be taken with slow and prolonged enjoyment.

Appropriately, we will start in the kitchen, with Slow Food. To escape the tediousness of "fast-food", let us rediscover the rich varieties and aromas of local cuisines.

In the name of productivity, the "fast life" has changed our lifestyle and now threatens our environment and our land (and city) scapes. Slow Food is the alternative, the avant-garde's riposte.

Real culture is here to be found. First of all, we can begin by cultivating taste, rather than impoverishing it, by stimulating progress, by encouraging international exchange programs, by endorsing worthwhile projects, by advocating historical food culture and by defending old-fashioned food traditions.

Slow Food assures us of a better quality lifestyle. With a snail purposely chosen as its patron and symbol, it is an idea and a way of life that needs much sure but steady support.

---

species that gives food its true flavour-spectrum, an activity coined by Petrini as "eco-gastronomy". Slow Food began promoting and finding markets for local, tasty, low-yielding species like the Piedmont cow and *otto file* corn (local-made into delicious bread), and so saving them from culinary – and biological – oblivion. Over the next five years the project became so popular that the organisation's members tripled.

The eco-gastronomy project has now evolved into the Ark of Taste, a catalogue of endangered flavours and products from around the world, like Noto almonds in Sicily or North American Navajo-Churro sheep. To preserve them, Slow Food links up local producer-networks (presidia) with interested consumers, sometimes when they are on opposite sides of the world. From providing a Santorini bean grower with marketing advice on

how he ply his wares or by getting producers and buyers together at Slow Food's huge annual food fair, the Salone del Gusto in Turin, the movement has found an ingenious way to set ethnicity and globalisation in a mutually beneficial relationship.

It's easy to see, though, why signing up to this Holy Grail of taste can feel uncomfortable to the Brits – skepticism is our tradition. But in our hyper-productive race we need all the visions we can get. ◉

www.slowfood.com

GO FOR IT!

An extract from *The Idle Thoughts of an Idle Fellow*
of 1886, by the peerless Jerome K. Jerome.
Illustrations by Tanya Ling

N ot exactly the sort of thing for an idle fellow to think about, is it? But outsiders, you know, often see most of the game; and sitting in my arbor by the wayside, smoking my hookah of contentment and eating the sweet lotus-leaves of indolence, I can look out musingly upon the whirling throng that rolls and tumbles past me on the great high-road of life.

Never-ending is the wild procession. Day and night you can hear the quick tramp of the myriad feet—some running, some walking, some halting and lame; but all hastening, all eager in the feverish race, all straining life and limb and heart and soul to reach the ever-receding horizon of success.

Mark them as they surge along—men and women, old and young, gentle and simple, fair and foul, rich and poor, merry and sad—all hurrying, bustling, scrambling. The strong pushing aside the weak, the cunning creeping past the foolish; those behind elbowing those before; those in front kicking, as they run, at those behind. Look close and see the flitting show. Here is an old man panting for breath, and there a timid maiden driven by a hard and sharp-faced matron; here is a studious youth, reading "How to Get On in the World" and letting everybody pass him as he stumbles along with his eyes on his book; here is a bored-looking man, with a fashionably dressed woman jogging his elbow; here a boy gazing wistfully back at the sunny village that he never again will see; here, with a firm and easy step, strides a broad-shouldered man; and here, with stealthy tread, a thin-faced, stooping fellow dodges and shuffles upon his way; here, with gaze fixed always on the ground, an artful rogue carefully works his way from side to side of the road and thinks he is going forward; and here a youth with a noble face stands, hesitating as he looks from the distant goal to the mud beneath his feet.

And now into sight comes a fair girl, with her dainty face growing more wrinkled at every step, and now a care-worn man, and now a hopeful lad.

A motley throng—a motley throng! Prince and beggar, sinner and saint, butcher and baker and candlestick maker, tinkers and tailors, and ploughboys and sailors—all jostling along together. Here the counsel in his wig and gown, and here the old Jew clothes-man under his dingy tiara; here the soldier in his scarlet, and here the undertaker's mute in streaming hat-band and worn cotton gloves; here the musty scholar fumbling his faded leaves, and here the scented actor dangling his showy seals. Here the glib politician crying his legislative panaceas, and here the peripatetic Cheap-Jack holding aloft his quack cures for human ills. Here the sleek capitalist and there the sinewy labourer; here the man of science and here the shoe-back; here the poet and here the water-rate collector; here the cabinet minister and there the ballet-dancer. Here a red-nosed publican shouting the praises of his vats and there a temperance lecturer at 50 pounds a night; here a judge and there a swindler; here a priest and there a gambler. Here a jewelled duchess, smiling and gracious; here a thin lodging-house keeper, irritable with cooking; and here a warbling, strutting thing, tawdry in paint and finery.

Cheek by cheek they struggle onward. Screaming, cursing, and praying, laughing, singing, and moaning, they rush past side by side. Their speed never slackens, the race never ends. There is no wayside rest for them, no halt by cooling fountains, no pause beneath green shades. On, on, on–on through the heat and the crowd and the dust–on, or they will be trampled down and lost–on, with throbbing brain and tottering limbs–on, till the heart grows sick, and the eyes grow blurred, and a gurgling groan tells those behind they may close up another space.

And yet, in spite of the killing pace and the stony track, who but the sluggard or the dolt can hold aloof from the course? Who–like the belated traveller that stands watching fairy revels till he snatches and drains the goblin cup and springs into the whirling circle–can view the mad tumult and not be drawn into its midst? Not I, for one. I confess to the wayside arbor, the pipe of contentment, and the lotus-leaves being altogether unsuitable metaphors. They sounded very nice and philosophical, but I'm afraid I am not the sort of person to sit in arbors smoking pipes when there is any fun going on outside. I think I more resemble the Irishman who, seeing a crowd collecting, sent his little girl out to ask if there was going to be a row–"Cos, if so, father would like to be in it."

I love the fierce strife. I like to watch it. I like to hear of people getting on in it–battling their way bravely and fairly–that is, not slipping through by luck or trickery. It stirs one's old Saxon fighting blood like the tales of "knights who fought 'gainst fearful odds" that thrilled us in our schoolboy days.

And fighting the battle of life is fighting against fearful odds, too. There are giants and dragons in this nineteenth century, and the golden casket that they guard is not so easy to win as it appears in the story-books. There, Algernon takes one long, last look at the ancestral hall, dashes the tear-drop from his eye, and goes off–to return in three years' time, rolling in riches. The authors do not tell us "how it's done," which is a pity, for it would surely prove exciting.

But then not one novelist in a thousand ever does tell us the real story of their hero. They linger for a dozen pages over a tea-party, but sum up a life's history with "he had become one of our merchant princes," or "he was now a great artist, with the world at his feet." Why, there is more real life in one of Gilbert's patter-songs than in half the biographical novels ever written. He relates to us all the various steps by which his office-boy rose to be the "ruler of the queen's navee," and explains to us how the briefless barrister managed to become a great and good judge, "ready to try this breach of promise of marriage." It is in the petty details, not in the great results, that

the interest of existence lies.

What we really want is a novel showing us all the hidden under-current of an ambitious man's career—his struggles, and failures, and hopes, his disappointments and victories. It would be an immense success. I am sure the wooing of Fortune would prove quite as interesting a tale as the wooing of any flesh-and-blood maiden, though, by the way, it would read extremely similar; for Fortune is, indeed, as the ancients painted her, very like a woman—not quite so unreasonable and inconsistent, but nearly so—and the pursuit is much the same in one case as in the other. Ben Jonson's couplet—
   "Court a mistress, she denies you;
   Let her alone, she will court you"
—puts them both in a nutshell. A woman never thoroughly cares for her lover until he has ceased to care for her; and it is not until you have snapped your fingers in Fortune's face and turned on your heel that she begins to smile upon you...

Good people say that it is quite right and proper that it should be so, and that it proves ambition is wicked.

Bosh! Good people are altogether wrong. (They always are, in my opinion. We never agree on any single point.) What would the world do without ambitious people, I should like to know? Why, it would be as flabby as a Norfolk dumpling. Ambitious people are the leaven which raises it into wholesome bread. Without ambitious people the world would never get up. They are busybodies who are about early in the morning, hammering, shouting, and rattling the fire-irons, and rendering it generally impossible for the rest of the house to remain in bed.

Wrong to be ambitious, forsooth! The men wrong who, with bent back and sweating brow, cut the smooth road over which humanity marches forward from generation to generation! Men wrong for using the talents that their Master has entrusted to them – for toiling while others play!

Of course they are seeking their reward. Man is not given that godlike unselfishness that thinks only of others' good. But in working for themselves they are working for us all. We are so bound together that no man can labour for himself alone. Each blow he strikes in his own behalf helps to mould the universe. The stream in struggling onward turns the mill-wheel; the coral insect, fashioning its tiny cell, joins continents to one another; and the ambitious man, building a pedestal for himself, leaves a monument to posterity. Alexander and Caesar fought for their own ends, but in doing so they put a belt of civilization half round the earth. Stephenson, to win a fortune, invented the steam-engine; and Shakespeare wrote his plays in order to keep a comfortable home for Mrs. Shakespeare and the little Shakespeares.

Contented, unambitious people are all very well in their way. They form a neat, useful background for great portraits to be painted against, and they make a respectable, if not particularly intelligent, audience for the active spirits of the age to play before. I have not a word to say against contented people so long as they keep quiet. But do not, for goodness' sake, let them go strutting about, as they are so fond of doing, crying out that they are the true models for the whole species. Why, they are the deadheads, the drones in the great hive, the street crowds that lounge about, gaping at those who are working.

And let them not imagine, either—as they are also fond of doing—that they are very wise and philosophical and that it is a very artful thing to be contented. It may be true that "a contented mind is happy anywhere," but so is a Jerusalem pony, and the consequence is that both are put anywhere and are treated anyhow. "Oh, you need not bother about him," is what is said; "he is very contented as he is, and it would be a pity to disturb him." And so your contented party is passed over and the discontented man gets his place.

If you are enough to be contented, don't show it, but grumble with the rest; and if you can do with a little, ask for a great deal. Because if you don't you won't get any. In this world it is necessary to adopt the principle pursued by the plaintiff in an action for damages, and to demand ten times more than you are ready to accept. If you can feel satisfied with a hundred, begin by insisting on a thousand; if you start by suggesting a hundred you will only get ten.

It was by not following this simple plan that poor Jean Jacques Rousseau came to such grief. He fixed the summit of his earthly bliss at living in an orchard with an amiable woman and a cow, and he never attained even that. He did get as far as the orchard, but the woman was not amiable, and she brought her mother with her, and there was no cow. Now, if he had made up his mind for a large country estate, a houseful of angels, and a cattle-show, he might have lived to possess his kitchen garden and one head of live-stock, and even possibly have come across that rara-avis— a really amiable woman.

What a terribly dull affair, too, life must be for contented people! How heavy the time must hang upon their hands, and what on earth do they occupy their thoughts with, supposing that they have any? Reading the paper and smoking seems to be the intellectual food of the majority of them, to which the more energetic add playing the flute and talking about the affairs of the next-door neighbour.

They never knew the excitement of expectation nor the stern delight of accomplished effort, such as stir the pulse of the man who has objects, and hopes, and plans. To the ambitious man life is a brilliant game—a game that calls forth all his tact and energy and nerve—a game to be won, in the long run, by the quick eye and the steady hand, and yet having sufficient chance about its working out to give it all the glorious zest of uncertainty. He exults in it as the strong swimmer in the heaving billows, as the athlete in the wrestle, the soldier in the battle.

And if he be defeated he wins the grim joy of fighting; if he lose the race, he, at least, has had a run. Better to work and fail than to sleep one's life away.

So, walk up, walk up, walk up. Walk up, ladies and gentlemen! walk up, boys and girls! Show your skill and try your strength; brave your luck and prove your pluck. Walk up! The show is never closed and the game is always going. The only genuine sport in all the fair, gentlemen—highly respectable and strictly moral—patronized by the nobility, clergy, and gentry. Established in the year one, gentlemen, and been flourishing ever since—walk up! Walk up, ladies and gentlemen, and take a hand. There are prizes for all and all can play. There is gold for the man and fame for the boy; rank for the maiden and pleasure for the fool. So walk up, ladies and gentlemen, walk up!—all prizes and no blanks; for some few win, and as to the rest, why—

"The rapture of pursuing
Is the prize the vanquished gain." ◉

EAT UP

From livers with flava beans to babies and bodily excretions, John Nicholson reflects on cannibalism and coprophagy in custom and culture

Once steak and kidney pudding was a weekly treat, now it conjures up associations with horrors. Risky territory. Jack the Ripper ate a bit of one victim's "kid ne" and sent the remains in the post. Albert Fish, who was caught and executed in 1936, wrote to the parents of the 12 year old girl he kidnapped, killed and ate. He didn't have normal sex with her, he consumed her in a cannibalistic union. Eating cooked strips of her flesh, with vegetables, "kept him in a continual state of sexual excitement".

DER KINDERFRESSER OR CHILD GUZZLER (HANS WEIDITZ, 16TH CENTURY)

Eating children is a favourite theme in stories told to chidlren

Transgressive connoisseurship is alive and well, thanks to Hannibal the Cannibal. His catchphrase: "I ate his liver with some fava beans and a light Chianti" finishes with a scary flourish of rat-like nibbling and chittering. The proverbial gnashing of demonic teeth.

For the ultimate taboo is against eating your own species. Ceremonial feasts in many parts of the world offer evidence of the opposite imperative. A victor ate parts of the vanquished to ensure his triumph, usually the heart or brain, to ingest his "mana" or spirit. Such necrophiliac transference, an embodiment, could lead to an after life.

The British empire was obsessed with cannibalism. Missionaries flexed their imaginations to fill heathen continents with cooking pots stewing appetising human dishes. Recipes increased the horror. "Jeane was cooking the flesh with congo beans, small and rather bitter, whilst Floreal put the head into a pot with yams to make some soup." One impatient, greedy assistant cut a slice from the child's palm to eat raw. Some tribes favoured palms, fingers and toes; others swore by the heart, thighs and upper arms. Deluges of such scares proved the need for a civilizing mission. Instead savages ought to be clothed, shown the error of their ways, be brought to true religion and accept the Eucharist.

Swift used this atavisitic horror for satirical effect. Asserting a metaphor of cannibalism, he suggested the logical next step was to eat the children and babies of the starving. That not only fed the Poor but prevented them breeding. We may wonder how Hitler would have viewed such a proposal.

Eating children is a favourite theme in stories told to children. Fairy tales are obsessed by eating. "The child builds puddings in the air, instead of castles … palaces of apple-dumplings … pavements of pancakes …" Grown-ups are often more voracious. Wicked witches and step-mothers don't torment children, they cook them to eat. The Babes in the Wood, Hansel and Gretl, are trapped in the witch's ginger bread house. (Even her house is edible.) She intends to put them in her oven. Happily they do this to her. "Dishing up children in a pie (for their own father or mother to eat unsuspectingly) constitutes the sweetest and most savage revenge for Titus Andronicus, as it does for the prince's wicked mother in The Sleeping Beauty, or for Swan Lake's rival in the fairy tale, both of whom are foiled in the attempt."

And what are we to make of miracles that took place in Paris in 1727? A star of the circus of pious "convulsionaries" was Mlle Gabrielle Moler, a young girl of about eighteen who had for a year been so scrupulously clean in her eating habits that she refused a bit of bread which had been touched by someone else. Fasting on bread and water she progressed to ox bile alone. Eventually she settled for a diet solely of excrement and urine, exactly a pound and a pint daily. Each day

HUNGER, MADNESS AND CRIME (ANTOINE WERTZ, 19TH CENTURY)

she insisted on a fresh way of preparation, sometimes boiled, sometimes diluted with liquid from a mixen, soot from the chimney, nail parings and other loathly ingredients which were recorded in detail.

The girl thrived and her complexion grew lily-white. Her deportment was agile and gay. She added a new turn. Signalling for a container, instead of vomiting, she brought up quantities of milk. Witnesses favoured with a taste, remarked on its quality.

How can we explain the ecstatic mysticism of female saints? St Theresa was pierced by divine love but there were other more recognisable routes. St Angela of Folgino tells us that she drank with delight the water in which she had just washed lepers' hands and feet.

"This beverage flooded us with such sweetness that the joy followed us home. Never had I drunk with such pleasure. In my throat was lodged a piece of scaly skin from the lepers' sores. Instead of getting rid of it, I made a great effort to swallow it and I succeeded. It seemed to me that I had just partaken of communion. I shall never be able to express the delight that inundated me."

We know that the Blessed Marie Alacoque cleaned up the vomit of a patient with her tongue. In her biography she describes the joy she felt when she has filled her mouth with the excrement of a man sick with diarrhoea. Jesus rewarded her and she held her lips pressed against his Sacred Heart for three hours.

We hear from advocates of Urine Therapy that drinking piss brings immense health benefits. No such pious excuse is offered by those with more specialised tastes, from the fans of stained underwear for sniff'n'snuck, used tampons, or fresh menses. Discharges including snot and spit are highly prized by their devotees. Connoisseurs of sexual cuisine too, the French have recently found exquisite pleasures in watching teenage girls vomit. Films of American college students begin with the all-American smile then graduate to a look of apprehension and conclude by the undigested ejaculation. Presumably this erotic vomitorium overtakes the demand for orgasmic squirting. In the last cases we have no reference to any audience participation. (They will, Oscar!)

Less scruples are evident in the peak viewing series *Sex And The City*, whose female characters compare the flavours of their partner's spunk with as much diligence as they devote to choosing shoes. "His is so sweet!" Count the calories. Oral satisfaction was also the route taken in a real life episode which supplied the basis for the Japanese

BARBARIC BARBIE

shock-hit film *Ai No Corrida*. A couple's sex games climax with the female castrating her partner. She was found naked, wandering the streets, his disembodied penis in her mouth.

I n case these sexual tastes sound rare we ought to remember how vile drinking water used to be. The quality of London water was so notorious it caused outbreaks of cholera and typhus. This is the customary fear during starvation epidemics when conditions so deteriorate the water supply is contaminated by sewage. The diseases which swept through the concentration camps were provoked by this disorder while any urban disaster requires immediate steps to stop outbreaks. A main defence for drinking beer rather than water was that beer was safer, having been boiled.

Hunger and starvation drive the urge to devour. *Suddenly Last Summer* is a play about devouring, not only food but lives. Tennessee Williams created many memorable images of frantic feeding, from the poet torn and eaten by boys to scavengers on middens for undigested food.

To combine the elements of this survey we may point to stories where the lovers are so consumed by passion they express the desires literally. Carolyn Slaughter's *The Banquet* climaxes with such a love-feast while the ghoul in *The Sandman* keeps the object of his desire in the deep freeze. Cannibalism, glutinous cruelty and coprophagy are the regular menu at de Sade's obligatory orgies. All the food is transgressive. The lunch is always naked. Ironically these gregarious debauches are conducted in private. You have to be a select member. The etiquette ruling depravity is as strict and as formulaic as Bunuel's bourgeois dinner parties.

"An elaborate bureaucracy is established to govern the production and distribution of faecal matter in *The 120 Days of Sodom*. The victims are placed on special diets, to ensure the quality and flavour of the turds. Saint Fond will put Juliette on a similar diet, for the same reason, and instruct her how to take care of her health to safeguard his own. The libertines become veritable connoisseurs of the turd, comparing vintages and bouquets with the mincing pedantry of the wine snob." Even at murderous orgies you should mind your manners.

"There is more to coprophagy than a particularly exotic perversion." Angela Carter saw beyond de Sade's literal shit to a higher, or lower, purpose. "The libertines ... monopolise the elementary productions of the bodies of others and arbitrarily regulate involuntary physical functions. Their coprophagic passions ... reflect their exhaustive greed". Carter identifies the ethos of the coprophage. "His economic sense, alert even in the grip of passion, insists that even the waste products of the flesh must not be wasted. All must be consumed".

Conspicuous consumption reaches its perfect expression in re-cycling food. Instead of the food tasters described in Rabelais, who checked and masticated before their benefactors ate, de Sade has his characters eating the "food" after it has been digested and excreted. This perversion of divine essence was either the final defiance, or the completion of the circle.

Divine, the star of the films made by The Pope of Bad Taste, is remembered not for being a grotesque drag queen but for guzzling a fresh dog turd. ☺

TAKE YOUR TIME

What happened to the shorter working week?
Sean Butler on Take Back Your Time Day.
Illustrations by Hannah Dyson

In the early twentieth century, many thinkers wondered aloud what people would do with all their free time come the turn of the millennium. In 1930, the economist John Maynard Keynes, predicted that the steady accumulation of capital would compel them to face their "permanent problem – how to use [their] freedom from pressing economic cares... to live wisely and agreeably and well." He suggested that by 2030 they might still work three hours a day just to "satisfy the old Adam" in most of them. Bertrand Russell believed that the four-hour workday was already within reach for Britain, a state of affairs that would cause "happiness and joy of life, instead of frayed nerves, weariness, and dyspepsia." And as late as 1965, a US Senate subcommittee, echoing the common belief of the time, predicted that the workweek would dwindle to 22 hours by

1985, and to 14 hours by the year 2000, with vacations in the range of 7 to 10 weeks. Like most prophets of the future, they were wrong. But it is worth examining why things didn't turn out the way they thought they would – the better to perhaps help their predictions come true.

Certainly, the remarkable productivity gains of the past century – quadrupling in the United States, for example – would lead one to believe that we of the industrialized world should be blessed with ample leisure time by now. Productivity, after all, means less input (work) for the same output (goods and services). But it can also mean the same input for more output, and this seems to be closer to what has happened, as people accepted bigger, better, faster things – and more of them – instead of more free time. As John Stuart Mill famously wrote, "It is questionable if all the mechanical devices yet made have lightened the day's toil of any human being." They've just allowed us to do increasingly more within the limited 24-hour day.

Over the past thirty years, this choice for consumerism over leisure time has been especially evident in the United States. While productivity gains did initially translate into more free time, with work hours declining from about 60 hours a week at the beginning of the century to 40 by the early 1970s, hours have been creeping upwards again since then, accounting for about an extra month's worth of work per year now. Americans, points out Professor Juliet Schor in her landmark book, *The Overworked American*, are now working longer than medieval peasants did.

The US is the only industrialized country in the world without minimum paid vacation legislation. By law, Brazilians get 24-30 days off, French 25, Germans 24, and Britons 20 – even the Chinese get 15. In practice, the average is usually even higher. The American average is only 10.2 days after three years on the job, while a quarter of workers have no vacations at all.

In addition to minuscule vacations, overtime is rampant; three-quarters of Americans work more than 40 hours a week, and a third work over 50 hours. To cope with all that overwork, Americans are spending more and more on an ever-widening

range of goodies – from pills to tropical resort vacations to therapy. And they're not letting their actual income limit their spending – more people declare personal bankruptcy in the US each year than graduate from college.

In Britain – where work hours have been more or less constant for the past 20 years – people are working about three weeks less per year than in the US, with half of all workers on the job for 40 plus hours a week. But worker output per hour has been higher in countries with a shorter workweek such as Norway, France, and Belgium, than in America since the mid-1990s. This is likely due to the well-known link between work time reduction and increased worker productivity, as well-rested and healthier employees work more efficiently. Try telling that to the number one workaholics: the South Koreans. They work 26 per cent more than Americans and 46 per cent more than the least-working Dutch. Ironically, the rise of the consumerist ethic was in reaction to productivity gains. What should have been a cause for widespread celebration – the economy producing more than we needed – was instead perceived as the ill of "overproduction". Industrialization had reached a fork in the road – either cut back production, or stimulate demand. The road to increased profits was clear – people had to be convinced to buy more.

Shortly after the Second World War, in what could be the economic manifesto for the second half of the twentieth century, American retailing analyst Victor Lebow declared that, "Our enormously productive economy... demands that we make consumption our way of life, that we convert the buying and use of goods into rituals, that we seek our spiritual satisfaction, our ego satisfaction, in consumption... We need things consumed, burned up, worn out, replaced, and discarded at an ever-increasing rate." It is, in fact, misleading to say Americans "chose" material abundance over time abundance; more accurately, industry, with the help of advertising, diligently thrust the consumerist ethos upon the population.

Another argument for increased work time is that there's a stronger "work ethic" in North America. But Canadian Anders Hayden, author of *Sharing the Work, Sparing the Planet*, rejects this notion, citing the fact that the US got the 40-hour work week before most European countries, in 1938. Sweden didn't get theirs until 1973, and Sweden's one of the nations with the shortest work hours today. "These things," he says, "aren't written in the national character."

Instead, Hayden offers a different explanation: "People often tend to look at why the employee is working longer," he says, "but it's not, in most cases, the employee who decides. The pressure, for the most part, comes from the employer." The downsizing frenzy that swept the corporate world in the 1990s, accompanied by government cutbacks to public service workers, has created a much more competitive job market. The survivors of layoffs have been forced to pick up the slack, or lose their jobs as well. Because of certain fixed costs per employee, employers believe it's more profitable to work their existing staff longer than hire additional people. "What we're seeing is a polarization of hours in Canada," explains Hayden. The percentage of the workforce working 30 to 40 hours a week slipped from 56 per cent in 1976, to 46 per cent in 1998, "creating problems of overwork for some, and underemployment for others."

There's a well known link between work time reduction and increased worker productivity

Wages also seem to play a role in work hours; if a person is paid more, the logic goes, they often tend to choose more leisure. Conversely, if people are struggling to make ends meet, they'll willingly accept more work hours. Economic historians – over 80 per cent of them, according to one survey – agree that the reduction of work hours in America in the early twentieth century was primarily due to increased wages.

The rise in working hours in the US could, therefore, be at least partly due to stagnant wages. For 60 per cent of US workers in the 1990s, wages either fell below or barely kept pace with inflation. Meanwhile, in the final years of the decade, the profits from huge productivity gains, instead of being passed on to workers in the form of increased wages, were funnelled directly into the stock market. By 1997, the richest one per cent owned an estimated 40 per cent of the nation's wealth – up from 20 per cent in 1979. In a 1974 editorial, *Business Week* sized up this period of increasing inequality with ominous clarity: "It will be a hard pill for most Americans to swallow – the idea of doing with less so that big business can have more. Nothing in this nation's history will compare with the selling job that is required to get the people to accept a new reality." Fortunately for big business, the advertising industry was already well seasoned from its selling job with consumerism.

Whatever the causes of long work hours in the United States, many Americans have had enough. A coalition of like-minded groups and individuals from across the US and Canada organized the first annual Take Back Your Time Day this past October 24. The date, which falls about nine weeks before the end of the year, emphasizes the fact that Americans now average almost nine weeks (350 hours) more work per year than their peers in Western Europe. Coincidentally, October 24 also happens to be the anniversary of the date that the US got the 40-hour workweek.

Take Back Your Time Day is intended to make us reflect on "the epidemic of overwork, over-scheduling and time famine that now threatens our health, our families and relationships, our communities and our environment." Groups held upwards of 100 events in cities throughout the continent, with activities that ranged from public discussions with physicians and theologians, to improv comedy workshops. The movement was featured in *Time* magazine and CNN's show, *Money* – which did an internet poll of 8,000 people and found that 85 per cent thought they were working too much. The Governor of Michigan made the day official in her state, while the hosts of National Public Radio's popular Car Talk made an enthusiastic "call for inaction" on what they rechristened "International Slackers Day". Not bad for a grassroots effort with a budget of $7,000 and one part-time paid staff. "We're case studies in overwork," admits Time Day National Coordinator, John de Graaf.

He hopes that all the work will pay off and Take Back Your Time Day will follow the precedent set by Earth Day. "Within three years of the first Earth Day," he says, "all the US's most important environmental legislation was passed and signed by a conservative Republican President – Nixon. Our feeling was that if Earth Day could galvanize that kind of activity, then maybe a Time Day could really put the issue of overwork on the front burner."

Along with the explosion in material goods, there has been a blossoming of options for how to spend our free time. Any resident of a moderately sized city could easily fill their days with a fascinating array of classes, performances, volunteering, and – of course – shopping. And one doesn't even need to leave one's house in order to soak up all that the 500-channel universe, internet, radio, telephone, books, magazines, and newspapers have to offer. While it's good that all these activities are available to us, like consumerism, we have to learn how to say "enough", and make time for unstructured, active, creative play.

One obstacle to living a life with less money but more free time in our societies is that leisure has been highly commodified. Henry Ford, visionary capitalist that he was, foresaw this tantalizing possibility when he introduced the weekend for his assembly plant workers in 1926 – reasoning, correctly, that a full two days off in a row would encourage families to do things like take picnics in the country. Naturally, the Model T would take them there. Whereas in Ford's day, free activities like socializing, community dances, and church occupied the bulk of leisure time, nowadays, most people have a hard time thinking of anything to do in their spare time that doesn't cost money. As one French worker asked after his country's decision to go to the 35-hour week, "...what is the worker going to do with his extra leisure time if he has no money?"

Surely, if we put our minds to it, we can come up with an answer – many answers – to his question. It's only been in the last 50 years or so that leisure time has been subsumed into the great maw of the economic machine. For all of human history before then, fun was just something we did, not bought. As Keynes wrote about his grandchildren, "...it will be those peoples who can keep alive and cultivate into a fuller perfection the art of life itself, and do not sell themselves for the means of life, who will be able to enjoy the abundance when it comes."

"I don't think you'll ever be given spare time on a platter," says Ursula Franklin, a professor at the University of Toronto and author of *The Real World of Technology.* "If you don't take your time... and say something rude to the people who try to monopolize it, it will not come."

While some thinkers have found their leisure utopia in the

future, others, like anthropologist Marshall Sahlins, have found it in the hunter-gatherer societies, which commonly worked just three hours a day. And it's true the tangible results of reducing the work week in many parts of Europe over the past two decades have been impressive, and set a new example for the rest of the industrialized world. Perhaps the dreamers are right, and we will finally come full circle and work as little as our hunter-gatherer forebears – but with all the benefits of civilization now at our disposal. As Bertrand Russell wrote: "Hitherto we have continued to be as energetic as we were before there were machines; in this we have been foolish, but there is no reason to go on being foolish forever." ☙

THE MAN WHO ATE EVERYTHING

Leo Hollis tells the story of the eccentric geologist William Buckland, lesser known contemporary of Charles Darwin and eater of hedgehogs. Illustration by Sandra Howgate

When Charles Darwin was at Cambridge he set up his own dining society, The Glutton Club, that advertised itself as a place to experiment "on birds and beasts which were before unknown to the human palate" and promote the delectation of "strange flesh". In the first few meetings they feasted on hawk and bittern but membership began to dwindle after a evening of old brown owl "which was indescribable".

Later in life, Darwin's gastronomic roamings would continue out of necessity as the Captain's companion on the *Beagle*. Long voyages in remote areas made uncommon demands on the palate. While in South America he ate armadillo, which he noted "tasted and looked like duck", and a 20lb rodent which was the "best meat I have ever tasted".

The author of *The Origins of Species* was one of the many scientists who were of the belief that "if you can kill it, skillet!" In pursuit of knowledge he dabbled in flavour and out of necessity he chose variety. But Darwin was no contest for the most extreme gastronomic taxonomer of all time. Charles Darwin considered him to be a buffoon, and the history of science tends to leapfrog over him as a background figure. But the geologist, churchman and eccentric William Buckland wins

our applause for both his discovery of fossilised shit – coprophiles – and his attempt to eat his way through the animal kingdom.

He was a man who took his work home and his work tended to include dinosaurs

From the high and dry tradition of the Anglican church, Buckland (1784-1856) showed an unexpected relish for the far shores of scientific knowledge. He had little time for the miraculous and believed in the material world. Once in an Italian church famed for its weeping martyr, he paused before the dark stain on the flagstones, dropped to his knees and tasted it. "I can tell you what this is," he announced. "It is bat's urine!"

As a young man, he was the first man at Oxford University to teach the new science of geology (or undergroundology as it was nick-named). He was known to travel the country on horseback, his pockets brimming with stones that he picked up. He become so knowledgeable about the formation of the island that one night on the way from Oxford to London, caught out by the decreasing light, he was able to get off his horse, pick up a handful of soil, smell it and confidently proclaim "Ah, Uxbridge!"

Perhaps his greatest claim to fame, however, was not found in the lecture hall, but at home. He did not just reserve his energies for the exploration of caves or the definitions of Megalosaurus teeth. He was a man who took his work home and everyone around him had to suffer the consequences; particularly as his work usually included dinosaurs. One night he sat bolt upright in bed and turned to his wife and spoke those unforgettable, heart stopping words: "I believe that the Cheirotherium's footsteps are undoubtedly testudinal!" His similarly aroused wife joined him downstairs to mix paste on the kitchen table with which they made a cast of the footsteps of their pet tortoise. It was indeed identical to that of the dinosaur.

Home life with the Bucklands was never normal and absolutely never quiet. The place was a tip, a zoo, a museum and a study. Roderick Murchison, a student remembers visiting one day. "Having climbed up a narrow staircase. . . I entered a long corridor-like room filled with rocks, shells and

When a turtle had been purchased, Buckland gave it a swim and his son rode on its back

bones in dire confusion. In a sort of sanctum at the end was my friend in a black gown, dressed like a necromancer, sitting on a rickety chair covered with fossils, clearing out a fossil bone from the matrix." This was not all one could expect. On the sideboard were another mound of fossils with the warning "Paws Off!" attached to dissuade the younger Bucklands from fiddling. There were animals dead and alive: a stuffed hippo was in the entrance, cages of animals and jars full of toads.

Walter Stanhope, a fellow tutor at Oxford, recalls how, one evening, he came across some of the more unusual co-inhabitants: "I took care to tuck up my legs on the sofa for fear of a casual bite from a jackal that was wandering around the room. After a while I heard the animal munching up something under the sofa and was relieved that he should find something to occupy him. I told Buckland, 'My poor guinea pigs!' He exclaimed, and sure enough four of the five of them had perished."

It was not unknown for the menageries to spill out of the family rooms. When a turtle had been purchased for a banquet, Buckland gave it a swim in fountains of Tom Quad while his son, Frank, rode on its back. Frank also had a chance to swim with a crocodile that Buckland had rescued by throwing them in the ponds of the Christ Church quadrangle. They did not last long but were then put to good use.

It was a short distance from the quadrangle to the dining table. The most dubious honour of all was to be invited to dine at the Buckland household. The tables was always elegantly laid with carved saurian bones as candle holders. If the meal was sometimes disturbed by the children riding a pony round the room, it was a pleasant distraction from having to look down to the plate. Buckland used these intimate events to share his finest discoveries from his trawl through the animal kingdom with his guests.

Moles, he pronounced, were "perfectly horrible" but not as bad as a bluebottle fly. He would regularly offer his guests hedgehog, puppy and and snails. The anatomist Richard Owen was not taken by roast ostrich while John Ruskin regretted having to miss "a delicate toast of mice." John Playfair recollects with fondness: "the hedgehog was a good experiment. . . the crocodile was an utter failure." On one occasion Buckland and a friend experimented with porpoise. They took fresh slices from its head, fried some and boiled others and decided it tasted like "a broiled lamp wick."

Buckland left Oxford in 1845 to take up the job of Dean of Westminster. But his son, Frank, soon returned to Christ Church to uphold the family tradition. He did so with more enthusiasm than his tutors may have liked. He was known at school to perform dissections on practically anything that moved. He also ate them, becoming famous for the phrase: "Bring 'em back alive and ready to eat." He was not above serving "Kangaroo ham, rhino pie, panther chops, horse's tongue and elephant trunk". He once campaigned for the use of horse flesh in English cooking but after an all-horse banquet he had to admit: 'in my humble opinion. . . hippophagy has not the slightest chance of success in this country."

At Oxford, Frank filled the Christ Church quads with eagles; in his rooms he kept a chameleon that would perch on a wine glass, swallowing flies; a jackal that would disturb undergraduates with its blood curdling cries and his pet bear Tig that he would dress up as a student and introduce to some of the tutors. It was diverting to see two or three of the dons not knowing what to do for fear their dignity compromised. Finally Frank was told that either the bear could stay or he could stay but not both.

Unfortunately, William Buckland's best days were behind him once he had left Oxford. Although he pursued his studies and won acclaim, after a coach accident in Italy in 1848 he began to decline into a dementia that would last eight years. There were no more dinner parties and very few visitors, as he spent his days reading the Bible and penny journals. Before his death he made explicit demands on how he was to be buried – in limestone with a Aberdeen granite slab as a head stone.

The final irony is that that man who once claimed to have procured from grave diggers the dried up heart of Louis XIV and eaten it, was buried without his head. His son could not resist the chance to look and performed a dissection on his father's own brain. The body was interned while the head made its way to the Hunterian Museum at the Royal College of Surgeons in Lincoln's Inn Field. ◉

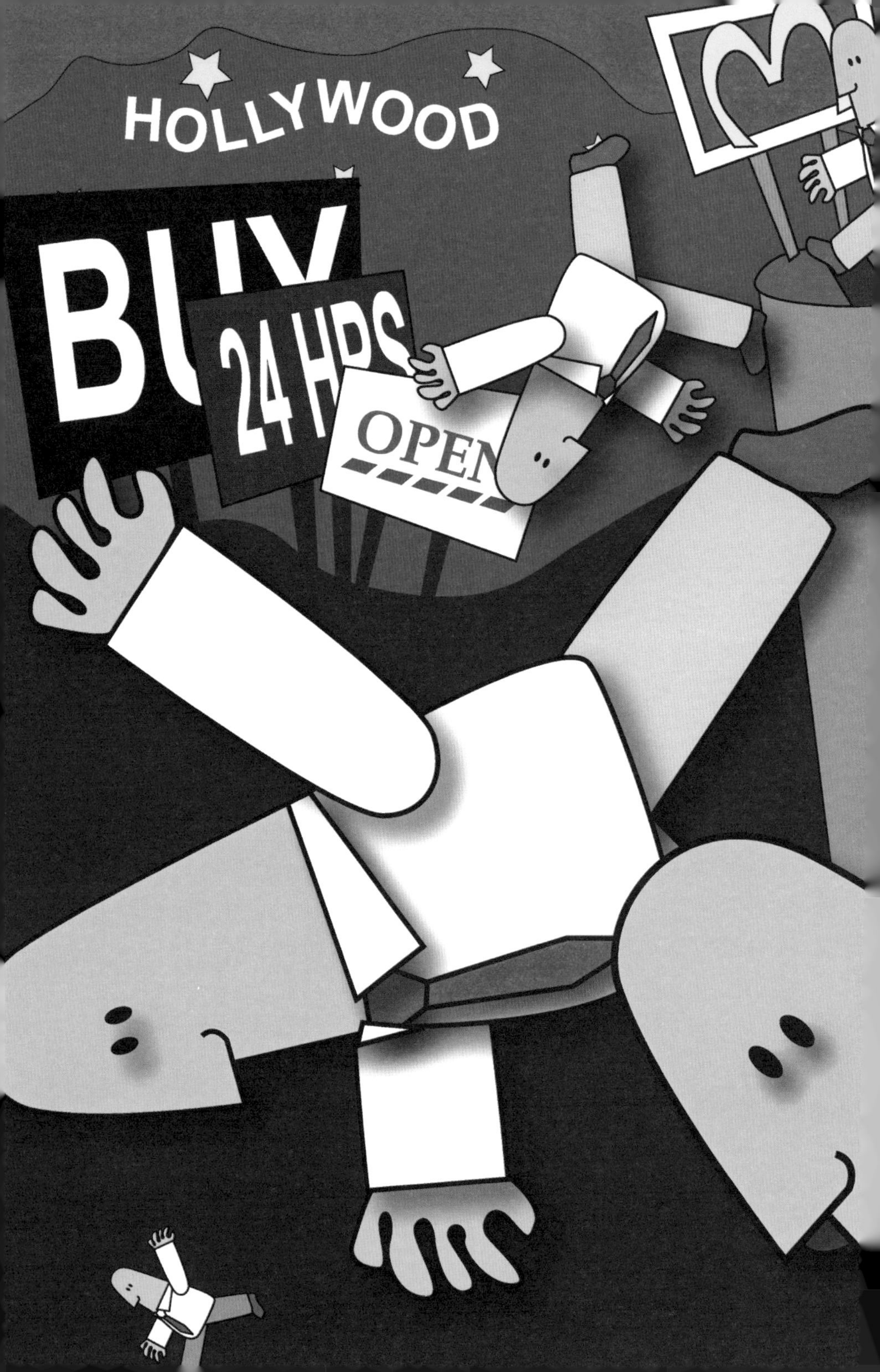
HOLLYWOOD

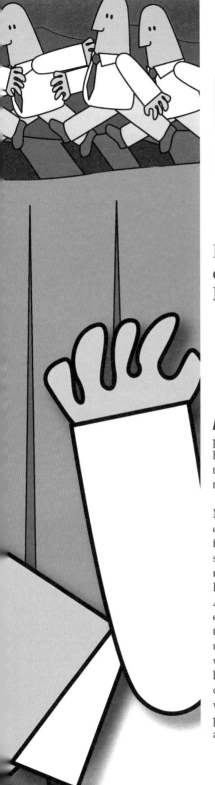

HUNGRY MOUTHS

Penny Rimbaud on why we can't get no satisfaction. Illustration by Sophie Lodge

As most of us are aware, behind every great man (sic) there's a cream bun or two, a tart and/or a mother. Nietzsche may well have bumped off God, but eventually a mixture of poor diet, bad company and too many hours at the quill put paid even to the philosophical Ubermensch himself; he ran back to his mum suffering a terminal bout of pox-driven madness. There are those who said that God had taken his revenge.

A prostitute paces the street outside McDonald's. She's sucking on her lips. There's a cold wind blowing in from the north. The twelve-fifteen from Darlington has just pulled into the station, and there's a carpet conference just up the road, starting in an hour or two. A man in a Burton suit crosses the road carrying a swatch of Axminster samples. He's got a twitch in his right eye, the effects of confused desires. He hadn't had time for breakfast, the missus has long since given up making any effort on his behalf. He may just as well have lived alone for all she, or he, cared. He's heading for the Golden M; it's a beacon. There's one in Darlington, maybe more. They're his watering hole. He likes the bright lights, the primary colours, the predictable smells, the aloofness of the staff; the blandness gives a sense of security, reflects his psyche. Warming his hands on the polystyreneburgerbox, he looks out into the street. The plate glass window is misty, lending the view a cinematic quality which he can't quite understand. He knows he's feeling something which is essentially European, but he's not sure what. He bites into his burger. A dribble of ketchup runs down his chin. At that moment the prostitute turns, dispassionately looks him in the eye, and involuntarily jerks back her head. It's an almost imperceptible movement, but it's enough to open the damp cellars of his mind. He doesn't know whether to finish his burger or take a slurp of his watery black coffee. As it is, he abandons both and pushes out into the street. She's waiting for him. He follows her to a hotel called The Royal. Later, at the conference, he apologises for having forgotten to bring along the Axminster samples; it had completely slipped his mind. The return journey to Darlington is uncomfortable. His seat is reserved, but there's someone in it. He can't smoke, so he reads the paper. There's been some kind of mass-killing somewhere in South America that he's never heard of, or maybe it's in Africa. Either way, it's got nothing to do with him. By the time he gets home, the missus is in bed. Supper isn't in the oven.

The fact that marriage is rarely much more than legalised prostitution (pre-nuptial agreements being more of a modern-day requirement than the registrar's certificate) does not detract from the truth that the physical hungers allayed by a prostitute are different to those satisfied within deeper relationships. Being bound by transaction rather than commitment, and thus being existentially removed, the oldest profession (like all of the newer ones: lawyer, banker, doctor, preacher, teacher etcetera) is abstracted from life itself: cum in number nine, your time is up. Uninvolved, arbitrary and unrelated, prostitution embodies the very essence of global capitalism: the choice is yours – "just do it." It all seems so ridiculously easy, but, put simply, that's because it is so utterly void of content.

The plethora of confused desires promoted by Hollywood, and eagerly adopted across the planet, typifies the deceptive techniques of capital and its insidious power to enforce and endorse what are no more than virtual realities. Playboy cheesecake was the sexual McBurger of its day, a de-energised polyglot drawing us into a semantic mire where we could all be President, could all fuck Marilyn Monroe and all kill a gook: a pre-post modernist deconstruction of authenticity. It is this continued process of deconstruction which ensures that we accept the indigestible counterfeits of fast food as a staff of life, or the needle-marked flesh of the prostitute as a giver of it. Like the prostitute, fast foods leave us empty. Like the massage parlour, supermarkets leave us bereft. Like the sex industry, corporate capitalism is dependent upon the effectiveness of its soliciting: "Buxom English rose will taste it and suck it before you spunk in her tight young pussy. American Express welcomed."

Within the construct of capital, food and sex are one of the same: natural, biological needs exploited and perverted into shallow reflections of what they might once have been. Punters return to the burger-bar not because they were satisfied the last time around, but because they were left so deeply unsatisfied. Suffering from this ambivalence, the only option is to return for more, which is, of course, less. It's a paradoxical work-out which somehow explains why the axe-man has to chop his victim time and again, and the squaddy is so casily driven into a frenzy of flying boot: more always becomes a necessity when, by nature, a quintessentially negative act proves itself to be unfulfilling. It is the circular, self-sealed world of the addict, constantly attempting to gratify a desire which cannot be gratified: chop, chop, boot, boot, glug, glug, puff, puff.

Like fast foods, the prostitute leaves us empty. Like the massage parlour, supermarkets leave us bereft

O f all the energies, capital is the meanest. While purporting to be a direct line to the "good life", it resolutely gives less than it takes, parasitically depleting the life-force, leaving us drained and confused. Be it through fast foods, sexual surrogates or the cynical jargon of the media, the nature of our existence becomes defined not by what or who we may be, but by what we are made into: helpless consumers consuming ourselves. Eat me, eat my dog.

Human action takes the form of its intention (woof, woof), which is to say that human energies should be judged not through the actions by which they are described, but through the intention by which they are driven. This further suggests that matter itself might not exist in material form, but rather in given or imposed energetic intention: the inanimate stone has, after all, no reason to walk, still less to talk. Nothing is what we see, everything is what we believe ourselves to be seeing, which is in fact what we have been conditioned to see: the fascism of form.

Matter and form are then ideological contrivances defined by the equally ideological contrivance of language: we can see no further than each other's eyes and can only describe what we see with another's tongue. Matter and form, being an expression of ideological intention, are then invested with a secondary level of intention, that being the one which we bring to them: our supposed, conditioned needs. Within this trap, matter and form are commodities which, rather than describing reality, reflect their ideological requirements of us as consumers. If we are thus not allowed to know our own self, how are we ever to know our own mind, and vice versa? By "buying in" to corporate reality, and thereby digesting the intention of others, we commit ourselves to their needs, our authenticity being energetically consumed by ourselves: the serpent eating its own tail.

Travelling through East Africa, I chanced to be in the back of a bush taxi with a couple of Masai elders. While I was fascinated by the vastness of the savannah through which we were passing, they sat immobile, their eyes fixed firmly on the rusting corrugated steel of the taxi's floor. Suddenly, far, far to the south, Kilimanjaro rose above the haze of heat and dust, its ragged icefields looking like cubist clouds carved into an otherwise perfect azure sky; I thought of Cezanne, Picasso, Alps, river basins, tide-lines and beaches. I thought of naked bodies in the sand, of the sun's heat on my flesh, of an arm reaching out to touch me. The elders hadn't batted a fly-covered eyelid. The diverse, albeit linear nature of my thoughts had taken me thousands of miles from where I was; while imagining myself to be concentrating, I had in fact removed myself from my situation. The elders, however,

appeared rooted to the spot, a manifestation of time and space. It was while I was musing on this that they became mildly animated. Firstly their noses twitched like dogs getting scent of prey, then their heads shook as if, rather than casting away thoughts, they were receiving energies. Then, looking up in perfect unison, they rubbed their eyes and through the torn canvas sides of the taxi peered out intently across the scrubby bush. Cows. For one hundred and fifty miles they had looked at nothing but the taxi's floor. Now they looked at cows.

The Masai have scores of different words for brown, about as many browns as there are cows. Equally, they have very few words for blue; the skies of Africa are, after all, predictably, and some say tediously, monochromatic. Cows are a Masai commodity, the sky's their giddy limit. Meanwhile, back in the UK the burgers burn.

Food is an energetic fusion; there's no food without an eater. At its best, food feeds both body and soul. At its corporate worst, while giving little more to the body than the discomforts of flatulence, it allows, indeed encourages the soul to wither. The food industry is not concerned with the preparation and marketing of food; its interest is in laundering money. In eating fast foods or processed supermarket junk, it is the energetics of money that we digest, allowing it to seep into every fibre of our body and soul: the lowest of food values, with nil symbolic worth, generating the meanest of energies deep within us.

Again, the key here is intention. Bread-making machines are as removed from real home-made bread as blow-up rubber dollies are from real sex. Yes, it could be claimed that rubber dollies, spongey pap or even Coca Cola are the real thing, and within the virtual reality of corporate capitalism they possibly are. Everything is contextual, but that is to ignore the all-encompassing nature of corporate ersatz. A friend who had survived Auschwitz once informed me that as a child in the camp, he and his playmates had used corpses to build dens. They were happy to do so and that was, of course, a reality. But was that reality the real thing? I would suggest not. Perhaps it is arguable that had that aberration had time to establish itself as a norm, it would have become an accepted reality, but as it was one in which most of its inmates were doomed to extinction, it should bear no further consideration. However, the question has to be asked as to just what degree the camps were a microcosm of what has now become known as the global village, or to what degree The New World Order is simply an extension of the holocaust agenda. I would argue that they are one of the same (known CIA and SS connections proving the point). All that has changed are the techniques employed. Systematic genocide carries on at a pace. True, its methods are different, but its form remains the same: violence supported through, by or with corporate capital (in a few notable cases, the very same corporate capital that financed the death camps).

In our mute acceptance of surrogate realities, we grow increasingly more physically and mentally obese. Bumbling around in a world of half-cocked ideas and shallow spin, we have become divorced from what little meaning words might once have had. Daily deluding our bodies and souls with the varied toxins of capital, we become incapable of making the choices which corporate capitalism likes to promote as a human right (most commonly referred to as "options"), yet knows to be a human impossibility, this being the very hook upon which it hangs its coat. Just as by reading newspapers we do not inform ourselves, so in digesting the cynical concoctions of the food industry we do not nourish ourselves. In both cases we are merely feeding the mouth that bites us.

As the power of Western religions collapsed under the forces of materialism, so the military/industrial complex, aided by the pseudo science of psychology, developed a corporate reality to take its place. Power changed hands, but, continuing to tow the line or, less euphemistically, tow the continuum, the fate of those who served

At its best, food feeds both body and soul. At its corporate worst, it encourages the soul to wither

those powers remained the same. The millions who throughout the twentieth century worked, fought, and died for causes and ideas which were not their own, did so both to further that reality and to ensure that it might stand unchallenged. Meanwhile, those whose causes they were, basked in the comforts of their mansions and palaces, stuffing their bellies with the fruits of our stupidity. We are, in short, trapped by the paradox of living our lives within a misanthropic reality whose existence is dependent solely upon our acceptance of it. Not only do we eat shit, we're taught to say thanks for the privilege.

Were we able or willing to comprehend that our own death will be an end to it all, a conclusive break in the continuum of the global soap-opera in which so much personal and social meaning is invested, we would be forced to realise that our life is uniquely and intrinsically our own. It is a responsibility which few are willing to bear.

Despite all that might have been or is yet to come, our existence is a self-contained event which should be defined not by the construct of corporate reality, but by our own will to exist. By removing the hypothetical contrivances of corporate reality from our lives (eat yourself, the kids'll like it), we become the creators of the universe, the purpose, the cause

and the effect. Indeed, we become the sole witness to this one lonely moment which is life. It is at that point we will have broken free from the consumer/consumed paradox of post-modern existence; we will, in fact, be free to make our own considered choices.

I recall daily watching an elderly German on an African beach. Early every morning he would take up his place where the sea met the sands and, until the sun set, he would stand, slowly turning round and round, cooking himself in much the way kebabs are prepared in Turkish restaurants. At first I regarded him with amusement, then with contempt; what a stupid way to behave. Then one day I saw him in the local market. He had abandoned his beach vigil to show off his tan to the locals, he by now being as black as the blackest amongst them. They were not impressed, and why should they be? They were black already. It wasn't until he slid down his trunks to expose the whiteness of his upper buttocks that he received the accolade that was his due. Now the locals were impressed. Some ran away squealing in delight, others drew closer, incredulously prodding his whiteness. Was he a black man with a white bottom, or a white man with a black everything else? No one seemed to be clear on this point, not least himself, but he had, I assumed, achieved what he wanted, and that, in today's world, is some achievement. It was then that my contempt was replaced with a reluctant form of admiration. So what had Nietzsche achieved that was any better than this, his fellow countryman? Nietzsche's foible was philosophy, it required hard work, dedication, commitment and no small amount of discomfort, exactly the same qualities displayed by our sun-worshipper. True, Nietzsche's works could be commodified (notably by the Nazis) in a way that the sun worshipper's couldn't (unless he was posthumously to be made into a lampshade), but did that in any way suggest or even prove anything about 'intrinsic' value? I guess not.

I've got several of Nietzsche's works in my library, and on my wall I've got a couple of photographs of the sun-worshipper. In one of them he is holding a stick by his side as if he has just beaten the young child rushing away to his right. Perhaps in his lonely vigil on the beach he too was a philosopher.

£££

The carpet salesman thinks of the whore at The Royal. He wonders whether she's been found yet. The missus snores her way through dreams of makeover, where nattily dressed cosmetic surgeons fork up slithers of smoked salmon from porcelain plates. Neither the carpet salesman nor his missus are happy, they never have been, but they're not unhappy either.

No different to the religious bondage which preceded it, commodity culture seeks to make victims of us all. Like lemmings, we willingly rush towards our prescribed fate. The supermarkets solicit twenty-four hours a day, Hollywood reigns supreme as a behavioural model, and what Sunday is complete without the psychic bile of Murdoch's minions? The neon flashes and the billboards bray. Garish geegaws, trinkets and trash (the cluster bombs of consumerism). Taking a toke is token freedom. Holidays beneath the ozone hole? Tits 'n' bums in Silicone City? One up the back passage of the sex machine? The red lights are always burning. Red is the new green. Trick or treat? Fuck or Flake? None of this is escape. It's a headlong dive into the stinking gutters of Mammon. ☺

Our life is uniquely and intrinsically our own. It is a responsibility that few are willing to bear

THE DEATH OF LUNCH

In this extract from *How To Be Idle*, Tom Hodgkinson mourns the loss of the midday meal. Pics by Marc Baines

I have a vague notion that once upon a time, not so long ago, lunch was a meal to be enjoyed. The midday meal was an occasion to be deliberated over, shared with friends and colleagues, savoured, taken over two or three hours. It was a time for gossip, laughter, booze. It was a dreamy oasis of pleasure which took the edge off the dreary afternoon and was to be looked forward to during the busy morning. It might even involve a stroll around town, a taxi-ride, a trip to a gallery. Sometimes lunch would go on all afternoon and into the evening, and leave behind it a delightful trail of cancelled appointments and drudgery postponed. "Lunch," wrote the great journalist Keith Waterhouse in his *The Theory and Practice of Lunch* (1986), "is free will."

But what does lunch mean now, to the modern worker in the twenty-first-century West? Sadly, lunch has been reduced to a merely practical affair. The tradition of the leisurely lunch has taken a beating from the new work ethic. Hence

the rise of the sandwich as the most efficient means of satisfying hunger with the minimum of fuss, and hence the huge success in the UK of "quality" sandwich suppliers Pret A Manger, who, with their French name, perky staff and piped jazz music, pretend to be "passionate about food", but are in reality more interested in stuffing the office worker efficiently in order for him or her to return to their desk more quickly. Their real passion, of course, is profit, and to create cash they have appealed to the culture of the time-starved worker. And in any case, any pretensions towards being passionate about food were surely revealed to be pure bunkum when the chain was bought up by those renowned lovers of quality, McDonald's.

We might lay the blame, indeed, at the feet of the busy, restless, striving Americans. Right back in 1882, Nietzsche noted that lunch was under threat from the new work ethic in the US. 'The breathless haste with which they work,' he wrote in The Gay Science, "is already beginning to infect the old Europe … One thinks with a watch in one's hand, even as one eats one's midday meal while reading the latest news of the stock-market; one lives as if one 'might miss out on something'." The death of lunch was an event more calamitous to some of us than the death of God.

Observing 1930s New York, Lin Yutang also complained that the speed of life was destroying the pleasure of eating. "The tempo of modern life is such that we are giving less and less time and thought to the matter of cooking and feeding … it is a pretty crazy life when one eats to work and does not work in order to eat."

This attitude to food, that it is a mere enabler of work, was carried forward by the fascists. Lunch, they believed, was useful if it increased production. Pleasure was not a consideration. The following passage is taken from an Italian factory-management manual from 1940:

> It cannot be a matter of indifference to the industrialist that his own employees should be more or less able to feed themselves appropriately while at the factory. As well as

The death of lunch was an event more calamitous to some of us than the death of God

considerations of a humanitarian nature, he should recognize that the function of food is to give the worker's body an injection of energy which will allow him to replenish that consumed by physical and mental effort, and to achieve and maintain as high a point as possible in the production curve, which as we know descends quickly when the worker has exhausted his reserves of energy.

The sacrifice of food to work reaches its apotheosis in the 1980s. In Oliver Stone's movie Wall Street, thrusting broker Gordon Gekko utters the immortal line: "Lunch? You gotta be kidding. Lunch is for wimps." Lunch meant wasting an hour which could be better spent working. Sociability and pleasure were off the menu. Lunch had been sacrificed to the great gods of work, progress and "beating the other guy". No one has the time to eat at leisure, it seems. It's a common sight to see people snaffling down a burger or sandwich between stops on the underground. This kind of eating has something almost guilty and furtive about it. It's not eating, it's lonely refuelling. The same thing has happened to breakfast. Handy little bits of solid cereal called "breakfast bars" advertise themselves with the slogan "Good Food on the Go". So much more efficient that way.

Today the workers' canteens have been privatised, and in the cities we eat alone, in McDonald's, Burger King, KFC and the aforementioned Pret A Manger. These are the places which today fulfil the fascist definition of the function of food, "to give the worker's body an injection of energy". It's a miserable sight, the rows of lone toilers sitting in the windows of these outlets, munching joylessly, reading the paper or staring blankly on to the street outside. The French philosopher Jean Baudrillard, in *America* (1986), comments on his sadness at the sight of another strange modern phenomenon – joggers – and then writes: "The only comparable distress is that of a man eating alone in the heart of the city."

In the UK and in the United States, idlers have witnessed with horror the rise of the Starbucks-style coffee shop, which is where many of us grab a lunchtime sandwich these days. The coffee shops of the twenty-first century have little or nothing in common with the coffee shops of the eighteenth century, which were loafing centres per excellence, serving vast bowls of alcoholic punch and existing to facilitate convivial exchanges. The modern Costas and Starbucks have as their secret mission purely useful goals: give you strong coffee and some bread to help you survive the day in a state of high anxiety and fear. They give off the unpleasant aroma of efficiency.

Hitting British shores in 1996, the first wave of coffee shops was led by the Seattle Coffee Company. At first, the notion seemed tempting. Squashy sofas, good coffee, soft lighting, yummy munchies. Admittedly, it was our own fault: the British café had never really got it right, what with its scorched instant coffee, cold toast, surly service, neon strip lighting, orange tables bolted to the floor, grime and charmlessness. So there was a gap in the market, no doubt. I remember being quite enthusiastic about them when writing an article in the *Face* magazine explaining the difference between a skinny latte and a double choco-mocha. The new coffee shops had a West Coast chic about them; they faintly reminded one of a beatnik San Francisco establishment; they looked like loafing zones, somewhere you could hang out, smoke and feel like a French intellectual. Could they be a gift to the non-employed?

But the cosy and entrepreneurial Seattle Coffee Company was wiped out when the vast Starbucks outfit bought all 65 of them in 1998, and these days every high street has its Costa, Starbucks, Aroma or Nero. Far from being loafing zones, these places are simply pit stops for working machines, petrol stations for human beings. As the writer Iain Sinclair puts it: '[T]he whole culture has speeded up so that people just queue to get takeaways. And it's the death of cafés. Who's going to spend days hanging out at cafés? It's gone.'

And what's the result of all this coffee-drinking? We're all wired. The UK is beginning to resemble the USA where drinking alcohol has been replaced by drinking coffee. So instead of being half cut all afternoon as in the days of the three-martini lunch, businessmen are wound up on caffeine, perspiring, worrying, rushing, shouting at junior staff and developing ulcers. I'm certain that we will soon discover the appalling effect of this coffee frenzy on the nation's physical and mental health. Truly, the coffee culture is inimical to the idler.

But not so long ago, in London and in New York City – those two poles of the work ethic – the leisurely lunch thrived.

'New York is the greatest city in the world for lunch ... That's the gregarious time,' wrote the humorist William Emerson, Jr, in 1975 in Newsweek. These lunches were seriously booze-soaked, too; the president Gerald Ford in a 1978 speech said, 'The three-martini lunch is the epitome of American efficiency. Where else can you get an earful, a bellyful and snootful at the same time?' And why has such wit and light humour disappeared from Presidential discourse?

Now if you've ever had three martinis you'll know that the effect is powerful. They are so strong that you practically inhale them. They make only the briefest contact with the stomach before entering the head.

Far from being loafing zones, Starbucks and their ilk are simply pit stops, petrol stations for human beings

Three over lunch must have led to the sight of some delightfully tipsy, not to mention big-haired and kipper-tied, statesmen and businessmen reeling into taxis on Park Avenue at 4 p.m., before going back to the wood-panelled office to loosen their tie, put their feet on the desk and give the staff the rest of the day off.

The 1970s was also a golden era for lunch in London. The journalist and writer Keith Waterhouse was a master of the art of lunch, and even wrote a wonderful book about it, The Theory and Practice of Lunch, published in 1986 when lunch had not quite degenerated into a mere stomach-filling exercise. In it, Waterhouse provided a lengthy definition of what lunch meant to him and, crucially, its pure use-factor was not among his criteria: 'It is not a meal partaken of, however congenial the company, with the principal object of nourishment ... It is not when either party is on a diet, on the wagon or in a hurry.' Lunch, said Waterhouse, 'is a midday meal taken at leisure by, ideally, two people ... it is essential that lunch companions are drawn together by some motivation beyond the pangs of hunger or the needs of commerce. A little light business may be touched, but the occasion is firmly social.'

Happily, the culture of the long business lunch thrives in some European countries. A couple of years ago I was in France on business to meet a firm of distillers. They were manufacturing a new brand of absinthe that my company had named and branded. About eight of us enjoyed a three-course meal, with snails, wine and absolutely no business discussed whatsoever. Just a lot of laughter. As the lunch went on and on, I started to get fidgety. Surely we should get back to their office, and conclude business? After all, we had to catch the Eurostar. But on voicing my anxieties, my desire to work was roundly dismissed by the French distillers. They laughed, arguing that there was no hurry, that things would happen all in good time, and they justified themselves with the following paradox: Travailler moins, produire plus. The less you work, the more you produce. They were right of course: the half hour which we had left to do our work was plenty. If we had allowed ourselves an hour and a half, then that is how long the job would have taken. Work expands to fit the time provided.

Anyway, this superb aphorism stuck in my mind. I might add that the whole incident was rather embarrassing for me, in that the editor of the Idler had been out-idled by some provincial businessmen.

But mutter 'travailler mons, produire plus' when you stumble back to the office at 3.30 and your boss upbraids you for slacking and you are unlikely to get much sympathy.

There is hope for Brits, and it comes in the form of the International Movement for the Defense of and the Right to Pleasure, more commonly known as Slow Food. Founded in 1986 by a group of left-wing Italians who were appalled by the cultural ascendancy of fast food, Slow Food's plan is to bring pleasure, quality, variety and humanity back to the production and eating of food. They do this by running events and tastings, and producing books and a superb magazine. From humble beginnings it has now spread all over Europe, with nearly 100,000 members. It has even recently opened an office in the US, birthplace of fast food. Their logo is the snail, and founder Carlo Petrini sees it as a "fully fledged cultural revolution".

As the Slow Food manifesto demonstrates, their philosophy reaches well beyond food, and can be seen as a protest against the dehumanizing mechanization of life:

Our century, which began and has developed under the insignia of industrial civilization, first invented the machine and then took it as its life model.

We are enslaved by speed and have all succumbed to the same insidious virus: Fast Life, which disrupts our habits, pervades the privacy of our homes and forces us to eat Fast Foods.

To be worthy of the name, Homo Sapiens should rid himself of speed before it reduces him to a species in danger of extinction.

A firm defense of quiet material pleasure is the only way to oppose the universal folly of Fast Life.

May suitable doses of guaranteed sensual pleasure and slow, long-lasting enjoyment preserve us from the contagion of the multitude who mistake frenzy for efficiency.

Our defense should begin at the table with Slow Food. Let us rediscover the flavors and savors of regional cooking and banish the degrading effects of Fast Food.

In the name of productivity, Fast Life has changed our way of being and threatens our environment and our landscapes. So Slow Food is now the only truly progressive answer.

That is what real culture is all about: developing taste rather than demeaning it. And what better way to set about this than an international exchange of experiences, knowledge, projects?

Slow Food guarantees a better future.

The British and the Americans are ripe for a Slow Food invasion. Long enough have we put up with food made by robots. The huge success of Eric Schlosser's book *Fast Food Nation* (2001), which describes the inhuman processes by which modern hamburger, chicken and French fry products are manufactured, and by the way revealing some of the appalling conditions and low wages suffered by the unskilled labour force which produces this stuff, is surely a positive sign. Perhaps we are waking up.

We need more lunches like the following, described in *An Angler at Large*, written by William Caine in 1911, when the pace of life was a little slower.

One eats with no sense of time lost. One's enjoyment of food – a very proper enjoyment – is not marred by any anxiety about the river. One lingers over the cigarette that follows and the cigarette that follows it. One does not hurry.

We need to claim lunch back. It is our natural right. It has been stolen from us by our rulers. The fear that keeps you chained to your desk, staring at your screen, does not serve your spirit. Lunch is a time to forget about being sensible, practical, efficient. A proper lunch should be spiritually as well as physically nourishing. Cosy, convivial, a treat; lunch is for loafers. ◉

STORIES

PARKER'S BAG

Fixated on fishing, Chris Yates tends to forget about food. Self-portrait by the author

I cut out a cardboard carp, tied it to the line from a centre-pin reel and lowered it out of my bedroom window so that it hung about six feet from the ground. Then I went to sleep. At first light, the reel screamed and I leapt out of bed. Jasper, calling to collect me, had seen the carp and given it a tug.

"It's more original than an alarm clock," I croaked, as I looked blearily out of the window.

There was no time for breakfast, though I snatched a cup of tea. I grabbed my bundle of rods, threw a few bits of tackle into a big bag, stole a loaf from the kitchen and away we went, driving through deserted lanes to one of our favourite waters.

The surface of the lake was almost invisible beneath its veil of mist; in the east the trees appeared hard and black against the increasing glow; all other details in the landscape were half-obscured by the combination of mist, dew and shadow. A fish leapt, making a big splash that we didn't see, but which sounded, in the midst of the dawn chorus, like a cymbal crash. The ripples spread, unseen under the mist, till they shuffled the reeds at our feet.

It was the perfect carp-fisher's dawn.

Jasper crept off one way, I crept the other. We had the lake to ourselves, though it was a club˅

"What do we need to make money for?" we said. "This midsummer morning is free, all we need is the time to be in it"

water. And we had the world to ourselves, though it was a Monday and we should have been working. "What do we need to make money for?" we said. "This midsummer morning is free, all we need is the time to be in it." Out went the offerings of loose crust and, within minutes, there was some enthusiastic clooping. Over in the weed bed, a bit of bread disappeared into a funnel-shaped mouth. I baited a size six hook with a crust the size of a matchbox and flicked it out. Two other free offerings went down before the carp approached the bait. He bumped it with his nose, turned, circled, sniffed again then just hung there, looking. His confidence and his appetite grew. He pushed the bread once, then took it in a single gulp. I waited until the line was slithering across the surface and then gave the rod a bang.

Whee! Scraps of weed and a gallon of water went skyward as the fish slashed the surface with his tail and plunged straight down. He stuck for a few seconds, in among the tangled stems, then bolted clear and, luckily for me, launched himself into the open water.

When I saw him roll, just off the net, I thought I'd got a ten-pound wildie, but it didn't make any difference to my enjoyment when the scales read two pounds less.

So dawn became morning. A breeze drove the mist away, the first ripples appeared on the surface and the first drone of "civilisation" sounded from a mile-distant road. The sun grew warmer, but the carp continued to feed. Jasper got two nice specimens on flake and I had another on crust – a four-pounder. Still we had a lake to ourselves, so we decided to fish on until our solitude was disturbed. As the day progressed, I began to wish I'd brought something to eat. It's always the same whenever I go fishing. I'm so keen to get to the waterside that I've only ever got time to grab the essentials of tackle. I would explode with frustration if I had to spend even five minutes making a sandwich or a flask of tea. After four hours' fishing I normally start complaining to myself for being so disorganised and impatient. I tell myself that it is humanly possible to prepare a packed lunch before setting out – have I not seen, with my own eyes, anglers arriving at the bankside laden not only with enough hardware to start a tackle shop but with enough food to open a restaurant?

It wouldn't be so bad if I could count on my friends, but while they're often good for a spare hook or float, or some bait, it's rare for any of them to have even so much as a packet of crisps.

I tried to overcome my hunger by concentrating on a difficult cast. There was a carp in a small lily bed not far from the inlet stream. To reach it, I had to drop a cast over a tall bed of reeds, being careful not to overcast into another reed bed just beyond the lilies. After three attempts, the bait landed in the right place and, within seconds, the carp took it down with a casual gulp. As I hauled, he dived towards me and locked himself snugly in the nearest reed clump. I had to call Jasper to help; he waded out and, somehow, got the bounder in the net.

"Hardly worth it," he said, looking down at a three-pounder.

"Never mind that," I replied, "have you got anything to eat?"

"Afraid not."

"What! Nothing?"

"I suppose we could bake the carp," he said.

"That's almost cannibalism," I said, "and anyway, we've got no chips."

We knew we'd quietly starve to death if we fished on, but fish on we did, for the carp were still frisky and we hoped we might contact one of the elusive monsters. An hour later I saw an apple pie surfacing in a weed bed. Jasper said his casting had improved enormously since he discovered that the pond was stocked with chocolate Swiss rolls. But he couldn't hook them. I said we'd better go home.

A few weeks later, four of us set out on an epic trip to a South Wales carp lake. Naturally, we were well supplied with tackle and, of course, we took provisions – but not enough to last. We'd planned to fish for nine days, yet after three we'd eaten everything, and after five we'd spent all our money. On the sixth day the carp's hunger was so great we forgot about our own, but on the seventh we knew we'd have to resort to drastic measures. So, in the morning, after a cup of black tea, we had to forgo the carp and set off to the local river for some trout.

Trout fishing on the Ithon was not very remarkable that season. In fact we felt sorry for any regular bona-fide trout fisher. After all, if four hardened (starving) carp-fishers could manage only one trout between them, and that on a worm, what hope was there for the dry-fly purist?

It was my brother, Nick, who got the fish and it wasn't nearly big enough to share. We watched him as he gutted, cleaned and cooked it over a small fire. But we couldn't watch him eat it.

The next day, I remembered Captain Oates. He was the valiant member of Scott's Antarctic expedition who went alone into the blizzards so that the rest of the team might survive on the dwindling supplies. I followed Oates' gallant example, setting out from the lakeside tent in the early morning so that the others might better sustain themselves on

An extract from
THE IDLE THOUGHTS OF AN
IDLE FELLOW
by Jerome K Jerome
(the first new edition of this lost classic
since the 1950s):

" Tobacco has been a blessing to us idlers. What the civil-service clerk before Sir Walter's time found to occupy their minds with it is hard to imagine. I attribute the quarrelsome nature of the Middle Ages young men entirely to the want of the soothing weed. They had no work to do and could not smoke, and the consequence was they were forever fighting and rowing. If, by any extraordinary chance, there was no war going, then they got up a deadly family feud with the next-door neighbour, and if, in spite of this, they still had a few spare moments on their hands, they occupied them with discussions as to whose sweetheart was the best looking, the arguments employed on both sides being battle-axes, clubs, etc. Questions of taste were soon decided in those days. When a twelfth-century youth fell in love he did not take three paces backward, gaze into her eyes, and tell her she was too beautiful to live. He said he would step outside and see about it. And if, when he got out, he met a man and broke his head—the other man's head, I mean—then that proved that his—the first fellow's—girl was a pretty girl. But if the other fellow broke his head—not his own, you know, but the other fellow's—the other fellow to the second fellow, that is, because of course the other fellow would only be the other fellow to him, not the first fellow who—well, if he broke his head, then his girl—not the other fellow's, but the fellow who was the—Look here, if A broke B's head, then A's girl was a pretty girl; but if B broke A's head, then A's girl wasn't a pretty girl, but B's girl was. That was their method of conducting art criticism.

Nowadays we light a pipe and let the girls fight it out among themselves. "

To order a copy of this marvellous book, visit www.snowbooks.com or any good bookstore.
ISBN: 1-905005-04-0   snowbooks
£9.99

CLASSIC BOOKS...
What is *The Idle Thoughts of an Idle Fellow?*
FROM THE AUTHOR OF
"THREE MEN IN A BOAT"
Jerome K Jerome is a rarity: a truly funny Victorian writer. The famed author of *Three Men in a Boat*, he also wrote these fourteen lesser-known essays for aspiring idlers everywhere.
"Published in 1886, still relevant, still devilishly funny"—*Tom Hodgkinson*
"A little comic masterpiece" – *The Independent*
...REDISCOVERED

the few remaining tea-bags and one stale loaf. I hitch-hiked home and spent the next night in the larder.

On the last day in September, a few seasons later, Jasper again called for me at dawn. Barbel were our quarry and we got down to the Avon near Ringwood just as the sun was rising. A lovely morning, the meadows sparkling with dew, the air warm and moist and the river reflecting the first tints of autumn.

At about nine o'clock, we noticed a familiar figure approaching across the fields. As he drew nearer we could see he was traditionally attired, looking in fact like a typical Golden Scale Club member, in his Norfolk jacket, Irish-tweed hat and heavy brogues. He had a cane rod in one hand, a capacious landing-net in the other and a game-bag slung over his shoulder. There was, however, one jarring feature in his appearance. In his left hand, together with the net, he was clutching a large white polythene bag.

"Salutations, noble Parker!" we said.

"Greetings, fellow barbel-baiters!" he replied.

"What's in the bag?" I asked.

"Not telling," came the reply.

We fished quite hard throughout that day. I explored a jungle of overgrown bank, fishing places you had to crawl to or climb into before you could cast. I found a formidable-looking swim where the current took the bait round and beneath a massive half-submerged willow. First cast I got a tremendous whiplash of a bite and just clamped down on it and tried to hold it. For a few seconds it seemed I was winning, then the fish rose into the trailing branches and snagged me solid. Jasper, fishing small baits, had a few chub and a beautiful two-pound grayling. Parker failed to land a fish though, like me, he had his chances.

As I said, we had worked hard at the river, and around tea-time, I began to feel that familiar, gnawing hunger; once more I began to crave for things other than fish. I struggled back through the jungle and trudged upstream to where Jasper was fishing. Imagine my delight when I saw a kettle boiling merrily on the bank.

"I suppose you haven't got anything to go with this?" queried Jasper, as he prepared three mugs of tea.

"Don't even mention food," I said, "we might start hallucinating again."

Parker, hearing the clink of tea-things, came down the bank carrying his plastic bag. "It's a present from the Captain," he said (the Captain is his remarkable wife). As he unwrapped it, the sun broke from behind a haloed cloud, barbel began leaping in the river, voles skipped arm in arm along the bank, a swan sang an operatic aria, bells began to chime and all the grasshoppers in the field burst into spontaneous applause.

It was plum-cake. ☜

From Casting At The Sun *by Chris Yates, Merlin Publishing*

UP, COCKY, UP

In which James Parker introduces Cocky the Fox.
Illustrations by David Hallows

Tippy toe, claws on carpet, here I come. I do dislike a sleeping house – the watchful spaces, the half-alive furniture. And the electricity! Not good for me. I nip past the dozing fridge and my tail flares like a Christmas tree, outrageous with static. Up the stairs I go, beady me, seedy me. My robber's sack is full – I have biscuits and Quavers, a bottle of V8, a Red Bull, even a carrot for the rabbit - but there is something I must do before I leave. A need is upon me, and I always honour my needs. I stand at the foot of the bed on my spring-loaded hind legs and take a sniff, a sceptical sniff. Deep in their sleep, and deeper still in the heavy, consoling sleep of marriage, a man and a woman lie breathing. I'm getting a wild ripe tuna-like tang off his underparts. She's soapier, smeared with creams. I lick my black lips.

Ten minutes later, I see the woman open sudden moon eyes in the darkness, awoken by some tiny sounds, some glassy clinks and whizzes and - a sighing? – from the en suite bathroom. She listens: there are words being murmured in there, and quashed noises, and fumbling attempts at discretion. Something rolls and is quickly stopped. There is a guilty strip of light beneath the closed door. She elbows her husband out of the bed.

Naked, blinking, a hand over his balls, he limps over to the door and throws it open.

"Ach!" he cries. "Ach! Filth!" Ha ha! It's me, Cocky the Fox, sprawled revelrously there on the tiles! In my paw is an open bottle of Eau de Gucci and my thin chops are wet with it – I could drink this stuff by the gallon. Empties litter the floor. The light bounces off my blackberry nose. "Filth!" cries the man again, as if every nasty flickering thing he ever saw out of the corner of his eye is now coiled and condensed turd-like before him. "FILTH!" Raising myself on one elbow, I look at him with heavy dignity. "The extraordinary thing is," I say, "it tastes even better than it smells." But he has turned his back on me, shown me the humble jostling of his buttocks, and gone in search of something to batter me with. Up, Cocky, up and out the window. Fly like a dream into the coming emptiness of dawn!

Champion is white all over, and his eyes are pink as if the blaze of his own whiteness has injured them or made them sore

Back at the hutch, Champion is waiting for me in his haze of anxious rabbit-smell, pellety, throbbing in consternation. Damn rabbit! Don't I always come back? But it's his nature to worry. "*New day?*" he honks when he sees me coming down the garden, dumb panic italicising his voice, "*Snappy new day?*" Yes yes, I assure him, it's a snappy new day for the two of us, and Cocky has the goods. Champion is white all over, and his eyes are pink as if the blaze of his own whiteness has injured them or made them sore. He's a big bastard too, yellow-fanged, something of a monster in his rabbit way, but absolutely helpless. We share his wire-fronted hutch because the terrible fat child who's supposed to feed him never does. I shake out the sack and of course he goes straight for the Quavers, biting through the bag. I should have kept them out of sight: a carrot would be better for him but once he's seen those Quavers that's it, Schmidt.

Poor Champion. I came back from a jaunt once and there he is half-drowned in the back corner, soaked through, a real mess, blinking between drooped and sozzled ears, his fur churned, his meagre straw blasted about and walls of the hutch all dark and wet. What's all this, I say. Shivering, he tells me the story. The kid's only been trying out his new water pistol on him, his Super Soaker! Little prick – in my mind I can hear his shrill glutted laugh. Champion doesn't get it. He worships his owner, despite everything. "Could he be angry with me, Foxy?" he says. "Why would he do this? Help me understand!" Love takes many forms, I tell him.

The light's coming up. The ruptured dew-trail I made coming down the garden is glistening secretively, in black blobs and dashes. I twitch the long comma of my tail.

There's cold in our bones but we're both noshing happily. "Bout time I got us some more tuna, eh?" I say. "Is it Cock?" says Champion. "I don't really eat that stuff. "That's right,

Pomona: Hunter Davies, Barry Hines, Ray Gosling,
Boff Whalley, Clancy Sigal, Andrew Martin, Crass,
Trevor Hoyle, Bill Nelson, Fred Eyre: great writers here live.

www.pomonauk.co.uk

you don't." "Too salty." "Yeah." I sniff, sniff thoughtfully. "Reckon I'll get some next time out though." "You've got a craving." "I have, mate." "There must be something in tuna, yeah, some vitamin or something that you're lacking?" "A deficiency? Could be."

Then I hear a soft chinking and smell that chocolatey smell as Otto the next-door comes padding up behind the fence. There's one knothole in the grey-green slats, and his shadow comes and goes behind it, his looming pampered bulk. He speaks to us in his voluptuous James Mason voice. "Ah," he says. "Breakfast time." Shite, I think to myself. "The usual is it, boys? Full English, plenty of tomato, keep the tea coming?" "Go home and polish your chain, you poof. Eat your treats." "I've been smelling you for half an hour, Cocky. You're like an industrial spill this morning., "Fuck off." Otto laughs amiably. He's a rotweiler. "And how are you, Mr Bunny?" Champion looks like he's about to have a heart attack. "I see your good friend is feeding you again. Which bin did he knock over today, I wonder." "Ever hear of an honest day's work, Otto?" I say. "There should be a flag over that kennel of yours, a nice big flag with a picture of a tin-opener on it. Your crest." "Very clever," he says. "You're very clever, all you foxes. So witty, so hard to catch. I've been meaning to ask, What became of your mum, Cocky? She didn't happen to get cornered by a pack of drooling cross-eyed beagles, did she?" "Slave! Parasite! Bitch!" I'm dancing and spitting now. "Bitch? One swing of my balls could knock you out, chickenbones." "Traitor!" "Tinker." "Man-lover!" "Scum." "Cannibal! You know what's in those tins you eat!" I'll get over this fence one day, Foxy," he says easily. The quiet furnace of his breath is close to the hole. "And then – after I've had your man there for elevenses – we'll talk." "Anytime, ex-dog. Anytime."

I mean it, too. Otto the Rot is soft. I'll scratch his eyes out.

I'll feast on the folds of his neck. I live a lean life, I'm very very sharp. He's still laughing at me though, horrid laugh from the other side of the fence, so I get going on a can of Red Bull and do my best to ignore him. I used to have some clout around here, I used to know people. That's right – me, Cocky the Fox, on a first name basis with all the faces. Holiday Harry, gamest fox ever, was my grand uncle-uncle-uncle. He ran this whole borough. Oh the capers and the japes! "It's all a circus, Cocky," he'd say to me, "and if you don't know it, you're one of the clowns." Then there was Rumpy the badger, his muscle – Grumpy Rumpy, war-faced with his black and white stripes. Long snout, bite like a pig's, he could take a pie-slice out of anything. And of course Marcus (I called him Mackie) Viles, king of the stoats, another character... But they fished Holiday out of the canal one afternoon, eyeless and dripping, in a funeral robe of green weed. Rumpy, who loved him, was useless after that – faded away. And Mackie Viles took his tribe of wrigglers and moved out to the country. Which is where I'd be, probably, if it wasn't for Champion. Dawn is spreading around us, its lengthening branches full of cheerless sharp-toned birds. "Oh, difficult!" cries the rabbit, nibbling and moaning. "Oh! Not easy!" ⊚

THE RED-THROATED DIVER

Food flies in the latest instalment from the trials of
Jock Scot's drunken birdwatcher, Peregrine Beer

Wayne appeared, full of authority and keen to exert it, he absolutely reeked of catering college and some patchouli oil he'd picked up on his travels.

"You spat at my staff!"

"Calm down dear boy! Mere coughing fit, didn't realise it was in my gob. I apologise profusely for any misunderstanding."

Wayne was too undermined to calm down. Perry slid to the floor, taking Pedro with him. As they lay there in a heap Pedro began to giggle and pull faces.

Spittle was gathering at the sides of his mouth. Perry looked into his eyes which resembled the window of a spin-dryer, rather than the windows to the soul, and recognised a fellow voyager.

They rose from the floor together, assisted by Wayne.

"You guys are out of order, you'll have to leave."

"I haven't had lunch yet! You can't cast an invalid out on the public highway in this weather, it's coming on to rain. In this country we have such a thing as a bona fide traveller, and I am onesuch. Anyway the manager is a personal friend of mine."

Mal drained a yard of scrumpy and belched triumphantly, "Bartender, fill 'er up."

Wayne didn't know which way to turn. Although travel is supposed to broaden the mind, learning the seven times table had seen Wayne reach the limit of his.

"Where's the manager! I want to file an official complaint!" screeched Perry.

"Ah! There you are girls! Oooh scrumptious foody-woodies!"

Wayne was growing desperate and tugged at some of the ironmongery which festooned his head. "Look you guys, I'll find a private room for you, there's kiddies here!"

Out on the reserve the more gullible of the party followed Bill Oddie around from lagoon to reed bed. Through their field-glasses they observed Sheld Ducks, flocks of Dunlin, Knots and other waders. Oddie almost creamed his pants when they glimpsed a pair of Avocets flying away from them, as his clumsy approach put them up. His running-off-at-the-mouth commentary continued incessantly as he fell into his TV persona. His demented shrieks occasionally falling to a whisper, usually too late to stop his quarry from flying off into cover or the

distance. Poor Bill failed to notice that his "I know best" attitude was also scaring off any serious bird-watchers in the party and after an hour or so he was left with just two old biddies who "Oohed!" and "Aahed!" at his half-informed comments, thrilled to be in his C-list company. Nodding away, exchanging un-knowing looks, delighted that a TV personality had entered their sad little lives. Eventually they got tired and sat down in the lee of a sand-dune to eat their sandwiches. Oddie wandered on towards the mud flats, unaware he was now talking to himself. He turned round awaiting a response to some obvious observation, saw no-one was with him, and as a curlew called plaintively across the estuary, he felt terribly alone.

Back at The Hampshire Ham, Perry's party were sitting down to eat.

Once settled at the dinner table the hubbub diminished somewhat as they studied the menu.The Libertonis ordered large helpings of pasta-based dishes and salad, the Texans, true to form, had the T-bone steak with side orders of onion rings and mashed potatoes. Edwyn, the vegetarian option. Perry, eccentric even at mealtimes, began with rhubarb crumble and ice cream, followed by the Dover sole and chips, then potatoes and Musselburgh leek soup before calling for the cheese board. Huge portions were scoffed and the gay repartee picked up again as the wine arrived. Many bottles. Bordolino, Lambrusco and Asti Spumante were savoured then drained with relish. Perry ordered Irish coffee. Passing the port, he offered Helen a glass. "Not hardly," she replied, with a winning smile. This baffled Perry, what could she mean? It must be US campus preppy slang he supposed. The Yanks couldn't even spell properly, never mind convey a clear meaning when conversing in the mother tongue. He had been a keen linguistics scholar when he was at Brasenose College, Oxford during his brief university career. (Unfortunately, he was sent down towards the end of his second year when, during a drunken lark at his 21st birthday celebrations, he had taken out his Purdie's and proceeded to blast the genitalia off several statues in the sculpture court.) Poor usage got right up his nose, on his tits and gave him pains in the neck and arse. But he could almost forgive Helen her slovenly speech, he found her very attractive. She had a beautiful profile, all the way down. So he tried to control his irritation and burst into song; it was the old Ronnie Renald favourite "If I were a Blackbird." After a couple of verses Perry thrilled the diners with a dazzling display of virtuoso whistling and the final descant trills brought forth a spontaneous round of applause. He sat down amidst calls of "Bravo!" and "Encore!" and as soup spoons beat a tattoo on the tablecloth he feigned a momentary display of false modesty before rising once again to his feet. But before he could delight the diners with an encore the door opened and in came Oddie. "Ah! There you are girls! Oooh scrumptious foody-woodies!"

Perry was having none of it. "Out! Out! This is a private room! Get yer own dinner!" he screamed and threw a soup ladle at him. Oddie retreated under protest behind pudgy palms.

Perry regained his composure and decided to treat his captive audience to his favourite poem "Ode to the Red-Throated Diver", an original composition. But it was not the right moment for Perry to read aloud in his breathless, deathless verse. Excellent and renowned though his timing was in recitation, he had not chosen the right time to declaim. Understandable, for our poet no longer knew what day it was. As he attempted to squeeze meaning from his doggeril, his tightly-shut eyes did not see the mayhem before him as a good, old-fashioned food-fight took hold of the room of diners. An untouched Bakewell Tart momentarily caught the eye of Mal the roadie, just as his assumed bourgeois table manners lost the inner struggle with his Gateshead genes. He let out a roar, grabbed the tart, fondled it lovingly for a moment as a mad, piercing glint appeared in his bloodshot eyes. He roared out what sounded like "AWAY THE LADS!" and launched it, frisbie-like, from one end of the table to the other. The Tart seemed to travel in slow motion down and above the table, hung, spinning in mid air for a nanosecond, resembling a *Sunday Times* colour

supplement recipe page illustration, before slapstickingly disintegrating with a wonderful sexy sound on Maria's bounteous balcony. She could not have been more ecstatic had she been on the brink of a third orgasm, maybe she was. Edwin was laughing uproariously when a wedge of Brie tickled his tonsils. He chewed, then half choked, Brie was not his favourite cheese. Not to be outdone, he scooped-up the remnants of the vegetarian option on his plate and hurled the spaghetti gloops across the table in the general direction of a Libertoni, Carlos was the unwitting recipient of the delicious mess. It hit him squarely on his knitted brow, leaving him looking like a blushing Yellowman, as tendrils of pasta decorated his Hoxton Fin. Luckily for the cleaners most of the scran had already been wolfed but the combatants did their best with what was left.

Helen, too pissed to be surprised, flicked grapes into the maelstrom and giggled. But Maria entered wholeheartedly into the spirit of things by stripping down to her undies and clambering onto the table. There she executed a mean Watusiau-go-go routine while screaming "Hit me! Hit me!" at the top of her lungs. The lads were more than willing to comply. Soon, many direct hits were scored, mainly on her heaving, pendulous bosoms, you could hardly miss them, such was their

enormity, and a very pretty target. Perry's stentorian tones went unheard as whoops and shrieks filled the air, but he soldiered on, lost in a highland, avian reverie.

The manager, Al McQuiz had taken refuge beneath the table as soon as the Bakewell Tart arced over it, the better to protect his vintage Seditionaries suiting. As he crouched there, doggy-style, he ogled Helen's sleekly toned legs and was content. He felt like getting his cock out and throwing off a quick one, but thought better of it. It was time to get the band to Kilburn for the gig before anyone got injured. The revelry was brought to an abrupt halt when Maria lost her footing as her tootsies skidded on the gunge which now carpeted the table and an un-controlled stage-dive saw her land in the mosh pit of Perry's lap. "--- sits upon the nest" were the words on his lips as he returned to the dining room's surreal reality. "Well Hell-o" was the next line he spoke, taking it all in his stride like the Stringfellow's habitué he was. He nuzzled Maria's cream smeared cleavage and thought what a delightful end to a delicious dinner. Food for thought indeed. ☺

Ode to the Red-Throated Diver

O! Red-Throated Diver you are
Very rarely spotted or observed
Keeping well away
I was lucky to come upon a pair of
   you's
On the Isle of Raasay while
   climbing up Dun-Caan
Halfway to the summit
Though the light was poor and dim
Were a pair of Colymbus Stellatus-
   at swim
Your unusual shape filled my
   binocular lense
I shifted my position on the hillside
And strained to look again
You floated along a wee lochan
High up in the hills
Lucky folk may spot you when
   they're out walking
One of nature's thrills
You dip your bill into the water
Then look up at the sky
Dimly aware of the passage
Of a skein of swans before your eyes
Floating like a mannequin
Swathed in dior's finest
You call out coolly to your mate
Who sits upon the nest

THE PRACTICAL IDLER

THE PRACTICAL IDLER

Welcome to the Practical Idler. Beer and tea appear to be recurring themes for the seeker of the good life, and in this issue we present some superb writing by the tea master, Chris Yates, and an ad for a really good delivery beer company. We've also got the John Seymour pupil Will Sutherland writing about his school of self-sufficiency. Idlers look after themselves, you know. Fanny Johnstone's car of the issue is the London black cab, surprisingly cheap to buy, and Dan Kieran writes on the pleasures of falconry. And there's a new travel section, with pieces on Mexico and the Fiji islands.

YOUR GUIDE TO THE EASY LIFE

RETREATS:
REVUCA, SLOVAKIA

Will Hogan finds a
paradise of good booze
and free living

GOULASH, BEER, MOUNTAINS

Like many Slovak towns, Revuca exists in a sort of chronological and geographical stasis. Situated miles from anywhere, it's the odd combination of being urban yet utterly rural. Despite having had the glint of Western capitalism shined in its beckoning eyes, it manages by and large to remain a delightful nugget of chaste simplicity since the communist government left office in 1993.

What remains of the communist regime is a legacy of excellent features i.e. cheap beer, cigarettes, food, housing, healthcare and so on, but best of all, everyone was entitled to (and they all bought one) a chalet and their own plot of land.

It is here that our trip to Slovakia really came into its own. All the things you could possibly need for a self-sustainable life sit subject like, at the foot of these magisterial Chalets. The temperate weather and arable soil provokes the wonderful ripening of apples, pears, oranges, apricots, grapes, potatoes, carrots, onions, beans.

Each has an outdoor oven, which was vast in dimensions and imbues a divine wood infused quality to food. While the last embers of sunshine filtered through the trees, we cooked goulash whilst quaffing beer and shots of Slibovitsa. We looked out from the balcony, inhaled the crystal clear air and gazed at the breathtaking views: banks of verdant forests framed by far away mountains, not to mention the exhilarating and concerning sight of a bear munching on a dustbin lid some twenty metres away from the outside lavvy.

If you fancy wriggling free of the muddy vesture of decay that is Western civilisation it's a great idea to visit Slovakia. With eighty Slovakian crowns to the English pound, this is as affordable a utopia as one can dare to dream. ☉

TOP SLOVAKIAN FACTS:

They keep a fish in a bathtub and feed it for two weeks before Christmas to have as Christmas lunch.

At Easter time, menfolk throw water on the women door to door, then hit them with spoons

80 to one ratio is the Crowns to Pounds.

It has caves of Aragonite with rock eating Bats.

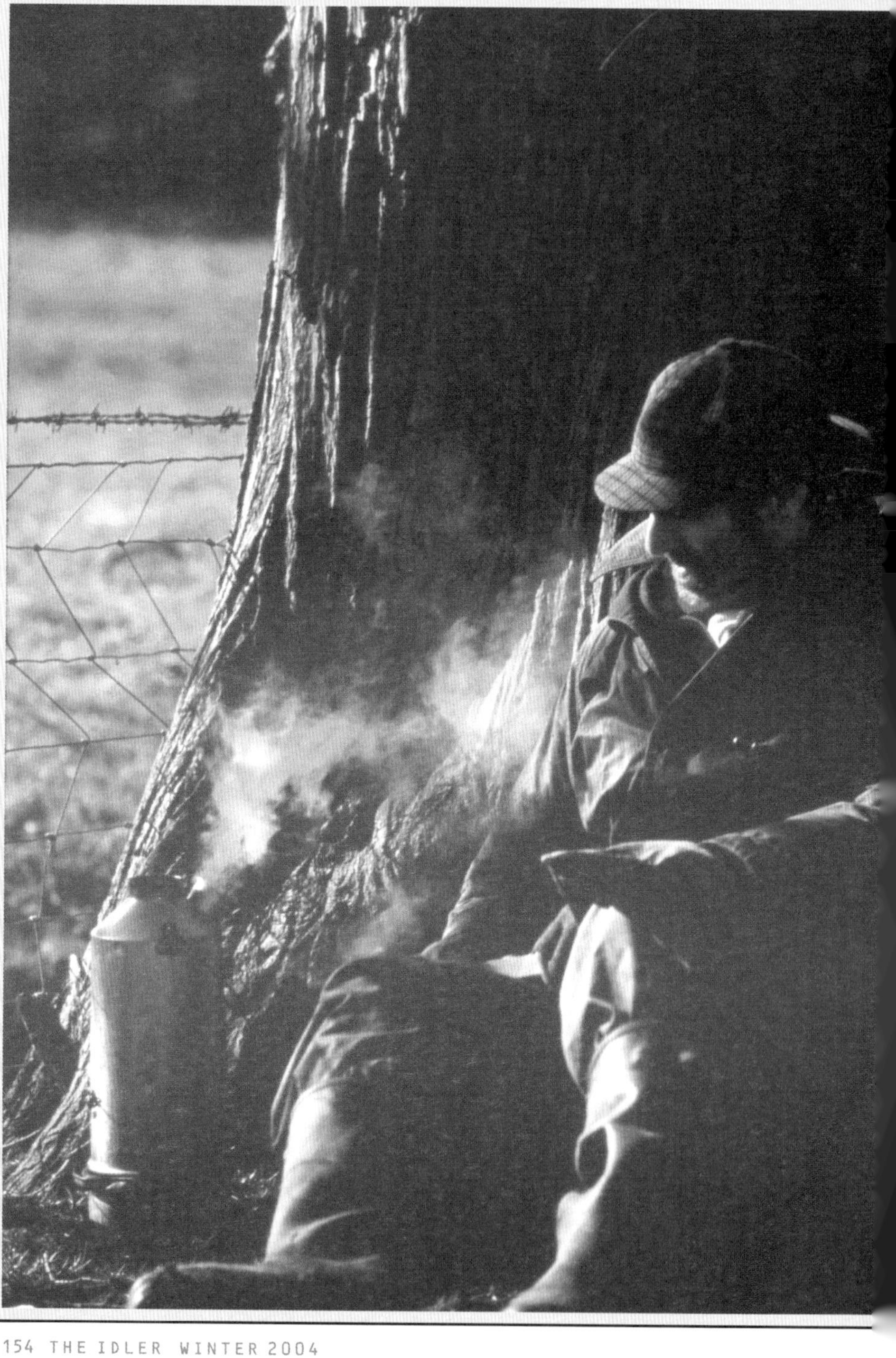

TEA TIME:
GREAT TEABREAKS OF OUR TIME

Chris Yates is out there

I think I have special powers, powers that are fuelled by tea.

Not long ago I was commissioned to write a piece about intuition and fishing. I began writing it on a train journey, not just because I happened to be going on a journey, but because I enjoy writing while travelling on trains. The only people likely to disturb you on a train are the ticket inspector and the tea lady. So I sat down in a seat by a table in a crowded carriage and took my notebook out of my old canvas fishing bag which I always carry about with me. For five minutes I tried to think of a title to my article. I looked out of the window, I looked at my fellow passengers. The man opposite me had his eyes closed, but didn't seem to be asleep. Then the tea lady arrived with her trolley and despite what I think about British Rail tea, I couldn't refuse her offer. Actually, the tea wasn't bad, though it needed the foil of an oatmeal biscuit. And it gave me the inspiration I needed. I wrote the title with a new confidence and was about to continue when the man opposite suddenly said: "I like your bag." (My notebook was resting on it). "It's just the sort of practical bag for the work I do. Can you still buy them?"

It turned out he was a professional dowser. But he didn't just dowse with a hazel stick for water, he also dowsed for elusive, far-ranging deer on large Scottish hunting estates. And if that was unusual what was even more interesting were the four words I'd just written.

"I'm a writer," I said. "You like my bag. How do you like the title for my next article?" I passed him my notebook and he read it out: "Dowsing With a Fishing Rod".

Now it's happened again. I wrote the title to this article while slowly savouring the first cup of tea of the day. I was in bed. It was about ten thirty when I drained the cup, but I couldn't continue with the writing until I'd made another pot. For some reason I went downstairs with the cup still balanced on my notebook, which was in my left hand, my pen still in my right. There must be a psychological term for my inability to put things down once my mind is focused, but in the kitchen I was distracted long enough by a dripping tap to put the pen on the draining board. This altered my balance by a crucial two or three degrees and the cup slid off my notebook and smashed to pieces on the tiled floor. And it wasn't just my cup. It was my best cup. Twenty five years old, beautifully shaped, Japanese, with an elegant decoration of two blue carp.

The connoisseur can boil himself dry extolling the virtues of First Flush Darjeeling, at ten pounds a packet, but the quality of any tea is vastly improved if you drink it from your own personal

A competition to win fine tea

We have teamed up with Grey's Teas to offer you a selection box of the finest loose leaf teas known to humanity.

There are eight boxes to be won, each offering a fine selection of teas from India, Africa and Ceylon, and each worth over £20.

For a chance to win a fine tea box, simply answer the following question:

What is a Pouchong tea?

Email your answer to will@idler.co.uk with the subject line "Greys Tea". Please state whether you would like Morning, Afternoon or All Day selection.

The first eight entries picked out of the hat on February 28 will win a Greys selection box, worth over twenty pounds.

Greys Tea are a quality tea merchants who deal in the finest large leaf loose teas in the world, offering a selection of over eighty teas. What's more, they wil deliver to your door for free anywhere in the UK. For Idler readers they will offer you a fifth packet of tea for free. To make an order, go to

WWW.GREYSTEAS.CO.UK

perfect tea cup - a vessel that may take you years to find. The diameter of the brim, the shape, the glaze, the size of the handle, the capacity are all important considerations, but you'll only discover if the cup fits when you've paid for it, brought it home and drunk tea from it over a period of time. And if it is The One, you don't do the sensible thing and rush back to the shop to buy a whole set of them, or even just the one reserve cup, because you know it'll be a futile exercise. There is only one One.

And now I haven't got my One any more. "Great Teabreaks of Our Time!" Why didn't I entitle this: How Nice to be Sipping Tea In Bed Whilst a Bag of Diamonds Comes Flying Through My Open Window.

It was my original intention to write about how a routine teabreak can change the course of world history. I had already chosen the photograph to accompany the article, a picture showing the author brewing up during The Anzio Campaign, and there is still a kind of relevance to it, even though the story is now unsuitable. It's relevant because it's showing a teabreak, but now I'm thinking that a teabreak can mean more than a mere pause for thought along the road of international events; it can also lead to something more mysterious.

Remembering the encounter on the train has spun my mental rewind back another few years to an even more curious tea-inspired meeting: Thursday August 31st, 1995: 'I went to explore an unusual house but, before I entered, I bought a cup of tea from a tea stall nearby. I didn't, however, want the tea immediately and asked if it could be brought to me after I'd explored the house. The tea lady - or, rather, tea girl - explainde that she was blind, but said that as long as I

first led her to the place where I wanted the tea she would bring it at the required time. "Once I've been shown the way," she said; "I always remember."

So I led her to a small doorway at the side of the house and agreed a time for her to meet me again with the tea. We parted and I entered the house through the front door. I realised the place was odd, that it had a disturbing reputation, but its darkness appealed to me and I wanted to immerse myself in its strangeness. And though the endless passageways and shadowy staircases were like a labyrinth I was reassured by the knowledge that the blind tea girl would be waiting for me at the appointed place and I kept the location of that little doorway clear in my mind.

Eventually, in a large gloomy hall, I met the owner of the house. He'd been waiting for me, confident that I'd finally arrive there.

"You knew what you were letting yourself in for when you entered here," he said in a deep calm voice. "Now I'm going to find great joy in your discomfiture."

Suddenly the shadows around us began to change. They became less broad, almost sinuous; the room seemed to be changing too, transforming into the interior of a wood.

The man remained standing in front of me. Elegantly dressed in a black suit and with round but firm features and dark slicked hair, I knew he had to be the Devil. But though he had power over me I had secret knowledge that gave me strength, despite him. I knew a way out through the side door, where a blind tea girl would be waiting for me.

(This last episode is quoted directly from my '95 dream diary. Now it's definitely time for another teabreak.) 🍵

THE ANGLER:
DO YOU FISH FOR FOOD?

Kevin Parr stands up for throwing in

"Barbel?- Are they good to eat?"

"Oh no, I don't eat them," I say.

"So you chuck 'em back?"

"Not 'chuck', more place, lovingly..."

"I don't see the point. Getting cold and wet just to pull a fish out that you ain't gonna eat..."

I normally switch off at this point. If I am in a sociable mood, then I may explain the deeper virtues of time spent by the riverside. But, more often than not, and this conversation occurs a lot, I smile resignedly and leave.

There is little value in arguing with an imbecile. If a person doesn't possess the gumption to appreciate the bigger picture, then you are not ever going to convince them with some whimsical rave about solitude and nature's companionship.

A recent conversation, however, prompted deeper thought. Zebejc (I think that is his name) is a former Bosnian working in IT who is forever smiling. We were chatting last week and he raised the subject of fishing. He was puzzled as to "coarse fish", and why, in this country we are so concerned for their survival after capture. I explained that many waters in Britain are pri-

vately owned and fish removal could be construed as theft, and, also, that due to the sheer amount of anglers here, fish stocks would rapidly deplete if we acted similarly to the Draconian laws of countries such as Germany, where it is actually illegal to return a fish alive to the water.

Still he was puzzled.

Why, though, the word "coarse", when many fish under this moniker are so good to eat? Indeed, back in Bosnia, he would fish for pleasure, but that joy was compounded by that evening's supper of chub or carp that he had fooled but an hour before. Even very small fish, gudgeon and roach, would be gutted and salted and rolled in flour, before being flash fried like butterfly prawns and served with fresh bread.

"So you have never fished for food?", he asked.

My father first drew my awareness to the possibilities of fishing for dinner. I was seven or eight and we were holidaying in a caravan on the Dorset coast where my father had grown up. My brother and I were itching to fish having discovered my father's old gear in a darker corner of the garage, and with good weather we found ourselves dodging adders in the bracken as we made our way to a favourite old fishing haunt. We walked for a couple of miles before dropping down a crumbling cliff path and onto rocky plateau which could have been created for rock fishing. My dad, sensibly aware of our short attention span, set our rods up with small hooks and baits, and soon our floats were dipping as baby wrasse and pout obliged to our enthusiasm. My father, meanwhile, fishing with a great big bait and stouter tackle, remained biteless. I spoke reassuringly to him, and suggested that if he wanted to catch fish, then he should ape our tactics. He smiled at my concern.

"I've caught plenty of small fish before," he

JOE HARRISON

Friends of the Idler, Living Beer.com kindly sent us hulking great box of ale. We then embarked upon the arduous job of sampling these fine elixirs and giving our thoughts.

Trembling rabbit
3.4% ABV
A twitching, zippy malt

O'Hanlons Wheat
4% ABV
Open-throatedly autumnal and cosy

White Shield
5.6% ABV
Patriotic and feisty yeast, with a rousing finish

Butts Blackguard
4.5% ABV
Burnt but lively Porter. An angry Guiness

Black Beauty
4.4% ABV
Doesn't spare the rod, Victorian in appearance and values

Royal Oak Traditional bitter 5% ABV
Sturdy fruit and pert lemons. An absolute cracker

Skew Sunshine
4.6% ABV
A cheeky climber. Hybrid home grown gold

Trafalgar
6% ABV
Velvet claw hammer

Nelsons Revenge
4.5% ABV
Swiftly climaxes. Serve after the Trafalgar for authenticity

Livingbeer.com deliver a selection of fine ales to your favourite quaffing chair. One can order specific denominations of ale, or simply order a specially edited selection box. We reviewed the Champion selection but others include the seasonal Christmas Selection, Cellarmans, Double Dozen, Bitter This, Bitter That and a multitude of others. Thanks to Tim Bryan, Sabine Rennefanz and Will Hogan. Order online or in person to Cellarman on 08700 460 557

explained. "But today I want a big one."

I left him to it, but felt some pity as the sun dipped and home-time approached.

I needn't have worried. Suddenly, my father was alive upon the reef, rod bent double as an unseen monster tried to pull him in. I remember being aware of feeling dizzy. In the sudden intensity, I had forgotten to breathe. My father was unruf-fled. He asked for the landing net and hauled up a Pollack so grand, I couldn't look at anything else. Now I realise that a Pollack of four pounds or so is no monster, but enough for a young family to make a meal of. And perhaps it was my father's heroism, or the fact that my baby sister caught a pound-and-a-half mackerel on the next trip, that prompted a deep rooted urge to fish for my family's supper.

A two-and-three-quarter-pound brown trout, caught out of season on a lump of bread from the river Itchen, was the first fish that I proudly took home. My mother assured me that it went in the freezer, but I don't recall it ever being served. Now, of course, I understand my moth-er's reluctance to cook such a ropey old fish. I was recently given a four-pound trout from the river Test, no less, which was, frankly, disgusting. The very thought of that muddy, stringy flesh is enough to make me vomit. Rainbow trout, along with farmed salmon, are unquestion-ably the most overrated of edi-ble delights. In fact, next time you are offered rain-bow trout, go outside and chew the earth for half-an-hour; it tastes the same, but you don't get the shits the next day.

I should, though, give credence to the natural brown trout of upper rivers, particularly upland streams. These are the same sources where water is bottled and sold for a fortune, and with fair reason, for it is pure and well oxygenated. Therefore the fish that live in such places are equally as wholesome, and well worth catching. A Highland holiday can only ever be improved by an early morning's angle in a mountain stream where the six-ounce breakfast trout are so eager to be caught (on a worm), and fit so well in a pan with a knob of butter and a twist of pepper.

I once ate a meal in the Hebrides which was entirely self-harvested – pan-fried highland trout followed by moules marineres, with fresh-caught dressed crab as a main. How much would that cost in Rick Stein's place?

The last time I fished with real purpose for my dinner was in august 1999. A horde of us were camping in my girlfriend's parents' hotel garden in Torquay, ready and waiting for an Eclipse.

After three days of continual debauchery, funds were low. After a campfire discussion, it was agreed that we all join Cyril, an old family friend, on a mackerel fishing trip, this being a clear source of both cheap entertainment, and, perhaps more importantly, barbeque fodder.

We ate joyously. The following night was again joyous. Nobody had to shop, for dinner was already arranged. Come the third night, however, and a couple of burgers sneaked onto the barbeque, peo-ple wanted variety. The fourth night, the night of the eclipse, saw a massive change of appetite.

I, for one, simply couldn't take it any more. On the third evening I picked loosely at the mackerel and ate only the bread with any relish, and, yet, here I was again, unpeeling tinfoil to reveal that unpleasantly familiar oily smell.

One mouthful was enough. I retched, threw my meal into the fire, and turned to befriend whoever it was who bought those burgers. 🕸

THE PASSENGER:
RIDING THE KNOWLEDGE

Fanny Johnstone sits in a black cab

Last Friday night, on my way to a party in Clerkenwell, I was thinking of my life in numbers versus coincidence. Was it possible that the party I was going to was the thousandeth party I'd attended in my life? At any point in history could the number of black-cab drivers giving out a receipt have exactly equalled the amount of black-cab drivers orgasming? What was the statistical probability that I'd be picked up by the same cab driver five times in ten years and would either of us remember the other? That's what I love about being in a cab. You can just watch London float by and mull over idle idiotic thoughts and not care if you don't get the answers.

I never tire of being in black cabs. I can attribute the slim silhouette of my finances to my fatcat love of taking cabs and as we trundled up Kensington Gore I wondered whether, like me, Nell Gwynn ever ran up debts by being endlessly carried around town in sedan chairs just for the hell of it.... loving the pitch and roll of being carried between two strong runners calling out: "By your leave, sir!" as they rushed up to street corners for fear of running into another sedan around the corner...a tad more polite than today's cabbies' calls.

The classic black London cab we've all grown up with is the Fairway. I love the reassuring rumble of its engine, the *droit de seigneur* type attitude of the black cab driver on London roads and the totally uncompromising curve of the seats when you're enjoying a passionate moment. In my world taking a black cab is synonymous with being on the way to somewhere fun and so, if I can lay my hands on enough cash to take a cab, I still feel amongst the rich and the free....

As we drove up Piccadilly I asked the driver (William) if he knew anyone who used a black cab as a private car and he said that yes, he thought Stephen Fry did. Which surprised me when I considered Stephen Fry actually driving rather than perennially lounging across Ottoman cushions comparing the colour combination of a khalim with his new cardigan. But anyhow apparently he drives one. I said to William that I shouldn't think Stephen drives the cab for the sheer spurious kick of Stephen-Fry-drives-a-black-cab, but that he exploits the black cab for exactly the same reason as me. For its ruminating hot-house feel. I can imagine Stephen now, trundling along Piccadilly thinking to himself: "Well of course Oscar would have been a fabulous cab driver. Oh yes. If Oscar had been alive today and short of a bob or two he would have entertained the masses with his wit while he drove, and rolled his eyes at everyone making hackneyed puns. Of course if Oscar had known who I was... that I was born to play him in the movie... he'd never have given me a lift for fear of our parodying each other to the degree that he would end up paying the fare. But if I had been able to pass anonymously into his cab I would have asked him to drive me 17 times around Hyde Park and Kensington Gardens in a figure of 8. Because I wonder... would Oscar do it? Would you chance it? Would you, Oscar...?"

THE
MAJESTY,
THE POWER,
THE FUN,
THE FREEDOM

And those are the kind of idle inconsequential ruminations that William and I decided Stephen would be thinking as he drives his cab up Oxford Street. Hey.... Oxford Street! Maybe driving up Oxford Street in your private car disguised as a cab wouldn't be the only privilege...

By the time we'd reached Holborn I've already worked out that if I owned a cab then on those insecure rainy nobody-bloody-loves-me days I'd go driving in my black cab just because I'd know everyone would WANT ME.

Or sometimes when I really hate the world I could drive along down the taxi rank at Paddington Station and, waving, go straight past a long queue and out the other side to annoy everyone.

Or I could barter for fares inspired by that time I had no money but desperately needed a lift to arrive punctually and intact for a date. The driver said he'd let me ride for free if he could moan all the way there about how much his teeth hurt.

Yes! If I had a black cab I could keep a pig in the back, or run a padded mobile crèche called Squeals on Wheels, or hire myself out as a non-conspicuous limousine to the FBI and CIA on their trans-Atlantic London-cruising frat parties with M16.....

As I said to William "Classic black cabs are the heart and soul of the capital. They're London's Easy Riders with Knowledge who'll open their doors to almost anyone. I want one." "You can have mine," says William as we roll down Clerkenwell Road. "You can have it for a grand." "Really? That sounds very cheap." God it was so cheap. How could I turn it down.... "They are cheap. The cabbies don't want the Fairways anymore. They all want the TXI. But the Fairway's very cheap to run too. 25 miles to a gallon of diesel, a babe to park, fully automatic, a turning circle tighter than.... and they'll bomb along quite happily at 70mph on the motorway with your entire family in the back." "There's only one problem, William," I said as I handed over the fare using my last £20 in the world. "I haven't got a spare grand because I've spent all my money on taxis."

An excellent website is www.taxi-mart.com. Taxis start at £400. The engines will generally be fine but watch out for rust. ◉

IDLE PURSUITS:
FALCONRY

Dan Kieran meets falconer Josh Flatman
Pictures by Chris Yates

I was driving along the north coast of Scotland last year when I saw a golden eagle on a rock a few hundred yards away. Well, I thought it was a golden eagle at the time. When I described it to a friend he told me it was almost certainly a buzzard. I felt a bit stupid, but was resigned to the fact that it was just one mistake of many I make whenever I try to identify anything in the natural world.

I can probably tell you three different species of tree by sight but one of those is a Christmas tree. I'm pretty sure what a blackbird is and a kingfisher but the varied wildlife and fauna of the country of my birth are, on the whole, a complete mystery. I know I knew some of those things when I was at primary school, but like Homer Simpson, all the new stuff I've learned since has pushed the old stuff out. And a terrifying proportion of the new stuff is utterly pointless. For example, I can tell you the last seven boyfriends of Kylie Minogue, I know that Jason Patrick starred in a film about a policeman who becomes a heroin addict. I know that Winona Ryder was going to play the part of Michael Corleone's daughter in The Godfather Part 3, but she was too exhausted and wanted

to spend more time with Johnny Depp who she was then going out with... and so on and so on. It's embarrassing and sad but I can't be the only one with all this rubbish filling up my brain. So I've decided to try and fill my head with more interesting things instead, like falconry.

To find out more about the life of a falconer Chris Yates and I visited Josh Flatman and his falcon, Cirrus, in Southern Wiltshire. Josh, who's twelve, lives in a converted barn with his parents and his sister Ellen. Out in the back garden they have an aviary where Cirrus lives. When we arrived Josh had Cirrus on a perch in the middle of the garden. I walked towards him nervously, but he seemed perfectly content as long as Josh was somewhere near.

CHRIS So what species is he?

JOSH He's a Peregrine hybrid with a Lanner falcon. He's 75% Lanner, 25% Peregrine.

DAN Where did he come from?

JOSH There's a breeder up in Stourford West. A real old time falconer whose been doing it for something like sixty years. And he bred him. I did a course in falconry up at the airfield.

DAN Had you wanted to do it for a long time then?

JOSH I'd never really thought about it, but I read about it in the local paper and went up there to have a look.

DAN Any excuse to get near a bird like that is a good one, I did a falconry day at Centreparcs and I couldn't believe how amazing it was. You feel as though you shouldn't be allowed to be that close to such wonderful birds.

CHRIS Into their space...

DAN But I read that people have been practicing Falconry for five thousand years! Josh, Chris was saying that the first time Cirrus saw a human being, it was you. How does that work?

JOSH WITH CIRRUS

JOSH Well, he was kept free in a breeding aviary and he was being reared by his own parents. It's important for a bond of trust to form between you and the bird and the first step of that is to try and make sure whoever will be looking after the bird is the first human it sees. With an owl you can hand rear it from three weeks old to make it tame but if you do that with a falcon it will think that you're a sibling, which can make it aggressive when it comes to food. So you go in, catch him up and you have to put the anklets on, which are the leather things on his feet, and you basically sit down with him for five hours a day. In the first week I had him on the glove for five hours a day, getting him used to me, then you try and get him to eat on the glove. At first they're totally nervous and they don't want to duck their heads when they start eating, because then they're not looking at you.

DAN So it thinks of you as a predator to start with?

JOSH Yes, we've got forward facing eyes so we're a predator to them.

CHRIS His eyes are so penetrating, and it's a wild pair of eyes too. It's calm, but it's wild.

JOSH He can see for about two miles accurately. He can see a rook or a pigeon two miles away,

DAN What do you feed him?

JOSH Day old chicks, quail, rats, you could feed them rabbit or things like that.

CHRIS We've got to have our tea, can we walk him over to our teacups?

JOSH Sure. The more mature he gets the more yellow his feet will get, before they were almost bluish, his beak will get yellower and yellower as he gets more mature.

DAN I read that they have yellow feet so that they don't eat their feet by mistake when they're eating their prey.

JOSH I don't know about that...

DAN I've read some weird things by the sounds of it. I bought this book that was written in the sixties about the memories of a falconer from 1907 and it says things like, "Falconry should not be practised when women are around because falcons can be put off by their skirts."

JOSH Who was that by?

CHRIS Cirrus, would you like a chocolate biscuit?

DAN I can't remember, it's really old but I'll lend it to you if you like. It's really, really funny. It's about this guy who used to go to Winchester College and he was driving home with his father when he spotted a falconer in a wood and from that moment he became obsessed. It has an index at the back and it's amazing to see how many words we use today that come from falconry.

JOSH I've got a really old book

from 1850 which is really good,

DAN So do you fly him every day? It seems like a hell of a commitment,

JOSH I try too. I mean when it's raining I can't. Most of the time I fly him every day. Except for when you fly them really hard, then you'll need to give them a rest day. [Cirrus begins to look agitated. To Cirrus] It's all right mate. He's looking for a higher perch; birds of prey are always looking for a higher perch. It's part of their instinct. [To Cirrus] It's all right, Cirrus.

DAN So are there exercises that you have to do all the time to get him used to you?

JOSH There are different ways you can do it, there's something called "tiring" where you get something like a rabbit leg and tie it up, so it's harder for the bird to pick at, you hold it and the falcon on the glove and walk about for as long as it takes the falcon to eat it. So while he's eating it he's being walked about, so he's getting used to being walked about on the fist. That can be quite stressful for a falcon. They could be sitting on the glove perfectly but then as soon as you start to walk it won't like the motion and it'll start to bate, freak out. It can be quite a slow laborious process really. Some people say that they can train birds in five days or whatever but it takes me a good few months. You need at least two weeks "manning" getting him used to you and the lure and things like that. Probably a month before you've got him flying free.

DAN It sounds like it takes an enormous amount of time.

JOSH It's something you've got to be trained to do. It's not a weekend thing.

DAN In my old book it said: "Hawking is the most difficult of all sports for the man without much leisure."

JOSH There's a builder I know who does all his building around his falcon,

DAN You need to be self-employed then by the sound of it. Is that something that you're going to do? How are you going to avoid work?

JOSH I don't know really, I'd love to work in the Highlands; I'd just love to work in Scotland, maybe

work on an estate or something,
DAN I can't imagine that there're a lot of jobs like that around.
JOSH No, not really. There're quite a few Falconry centres about, though.
DAN I went to the one in Andover quite recently and they've got some amazing birds.
JOSH I went there last week, they had a Gyr falcon that had been taken from Customs. Wildlife is the fourth biggest illegal trade in Britain after guns, alcohol and drugs. They've just arranged that any birds of prey that get confiscated by Customs will go to Andover.
DAN That sounds like a good end to a bad situation then. [Cirrus begins to ruffle up.] Is he frightened?
JOSH That's called rousing up, when they puff up their feathers like those on his head, and he's got a little beard under his chin. He's saying, "I'm relaxed, I'm getting air in between my feathers, I'm happy."
CHRIS His plumage is fantastic,
JOSH They have a very complicated preening system. Which they do after they've eaten when you put them in for bed.
DAN How come one of his tail feathers is so much longer than the other?
JOSH Well that's because in his first moult he was a bit inexperienced, and as feathers come through they can be quite itchy sometimes, so what he did was over-preen them, and he snapped some of them, so he's lost those sadly.

DAN, JOSH AND CIRRUS

CHRIS He looks like he'd be very good at turning right, but not very good at turning left...
JOSH (laughing) You'd think so, the first time I flew him I thought he'd go round in a circle, but he just uses his tail a lot, to adjust.
DAN So how do you train him?
JOSH You have to build them up for everything, because if you try to do it too quickly he'd most likely just fly off and sit in a tree. To start with you fly them to the lure, which is a leather pad on a length of line with a bit of meat on. You fly falcons to the lure and spin it round and then the bird flies in and catches it. A hawk should fly to the fist, with a bit of meat on. But the falcons, because they're more used to killing birds, need to fly in, hit it and then keep on hitting it until it's dead and that's why you use a lure, because it takes the bird back to it's natural instinct. You start off with it about a foot away from the bird and get it to jump on it and then you take it further and further away and then you might start hiding it and then he has to fly around a bit, and that's the stage I'm up to at the moment. He's up to flying two or three times around me before I get worried that he might fly away. Then I have to get the lure back out.

CHRIS How far away is he from you then when he's doing those circles?

JOSH Quite far and in big arcs because Peregrines haven't got the quickest turning circle, they're not that sharp, but the Gyr Falcons can turn on a six-pence. But Peregrine Lanners can't really.

DAN So what's the final goal?

JOSH Well, in the end the bird will get so confident that it just does what it wants really. It will go off and know that it can come back to you. Most of the time it will just stay above you, circle around you, go quite high, and build up its confidence so that it knows that you are it's food source. Then maybe one day you can go off and try and hunt something. It's the perfect size for partridge; it's a bit too small for anything else.

DAN Is it a popular thing to do now?

JOSH It has got more popular, there's about 2,000 practising falconers in Britain today. The hybriding has only really been started in the last twenty years or so. You have to breed them with closely related species where their genes are quite closely related, and a quite common mix is a Gyr Saker, and even though one lives in Saudi Arabia and one lives in the Arctic they're very closely related genetically.

CHRIS What would be the advantage, though?

JOSH Gyrs are very temperamental, but they're the most

highly prized falconry birds. They're the biggest, the quickest and the most powerful. But the problem with them is that if you're flying them at an airfield or something, they're so temperamental that they'd just leg it. So the saker will just balance it out. The Sakers are very greedy so they're a lot easier to train. They always want to come back because they always want to be fed. The peregrines can be quite temperamental, and they can be quite vocal as well, and the lanner's the perfect beginners' bird.

DAN So would you work your way through the species? I heard that harris hawks are the most popular to start with,

JOSH Yeah. Falcons are a lot more complex than harris hawks really. I just fell in love with falcons. I like the fact that falcons go off to do their own thing and when it's off flying it chooses to come back to you. However long you fly it. The harris hawk will just follow behind you like a dog.

DAN So how much does a bird like Cirrus cost?

JOSH He was £250 but they vary between fifty pounds for a Kestrel or barn owl because they're so common and easy to breed and they go up to like £12,000 for a female, pure white, Gyr falcon. £12-15,000.

DAN And do you have to have a license?

JOSH You do have to license hybrids because they're rare in the wild, well you wouldn't get them in the wild, but I think someone should have to come and check you out. But you don't have to register all birds of prey, the harris hawks you don't have to register, anyone could go out and buy a load of them; saker falcons you don't have to register, it's just dependent on their status in the wild. I'm just going to put his hood on; otherwise he'll totally sketch out in the car. I've trained him by feeding him every time I take the hood off so now he associates the hood with a reward, that's why he's happy to put it on. Once we're up the hill you can hold him and take off the hood, and then he'll see me and that will be his reward. That he can come to the lure by flying. Hopefully he'll behave himself.

Josh took us up to a nearby hill to show us

Cirrus in flight. I put on a falconer's glove and, when prompted by Josh who stood a hundred yards away, removed the hood and released my hand. Cirrus looked at me for a split second, launched himself into the air and headed for Josh. He flew in circles around Josh's spinning lure but decided to land ten metres from where Josh was standing on a nearby patch of grass. Josh ran over to him and by offering him a rabbit's foot, got him back on the glove.

JOSH We'll have to go back, I'm afraid. I've given him a tiny bit of meat but I'll have to come back later on. If I fly him to the lure again now he'll think, "fine, I still get the reward even if I fly off and sit down wherever I like" and I can't teach him that that's OK. So that's it, we'll have to go back home. I'm sorry...

CHRIS No, no, that's fine.

JOSH I think he was slightly too heavy, an eighth of an ounce too heavy.

DAN Really, is that all?

JOSH A bigger bird would have a one-ounce or two-ounce window, they might fly between two pound one and two pound three. He'll fly between one pound and one pound and a quarter of an ounce. With a kestrel it's even harder, you've got to be bang on.

DAN So because he's not hungry he can see no reason to fly? Because he doesn't need to eat, work has no purpose?

JOSH Exactly.

DAN That's the kind of work ethic I admire. ☺

FALCONRY PARLANCE

From Hartling's Bibliotheca Accipitraria
BATE, BATING, fluttering or flying off the fist, which an untrained hawk commonly does at the sight of the approaching hood. Literally to beat the air with the wings, from the French *battre*. "It is calde batying for she batith with hirselfe, most oftyn causeles." - Boke of St Albans, 1486
BOWSE, v., to drink; variously spelt "bouse," "boose," "bouze," and "booze."
CADGER, the person who carries the hawk; hence the abbreviated form "cad", a person fit for no other occupation.
LURE, a bait. Technically, a bunch of feathers, or couple of wings tied together on a piece of leather, and weighted. Being garnished with raw meat, the hawk is always fed upon it. Hence, when swung aloft, it serves to lure the hawk back to the falconer.
PREEN, v., to dress the feathers with the beak.
STOOP, s., the swift descent of a falcon on the quarry from a height; synonymous with swoop.

Further reading: The Goshawk *by T.H. White*, A Manual of Falconry *by M.H. Woodford*, Falconry *by Jemima Parry-Jones*

IDLE PURSUITS:
B&B ETIQUETTE

Gavin Pretor-Pinney has some tips

There is nowhere quite like the breakfast room of a British B&B. The guests look up from their mini jam cartons with a sheepish grin, as you come in and take your seat. Conversations are conducted at a whisper, punctuated only by the clink of cutlery and the owner's simpering descriptions of the fare.

All strained environments rely on a strict code of conduct. And the B&B breakfast is no different. Perhaps you just came for a dirty weekend with your lover, but you'll ignore this lace-and-chinz etiquette at your peril, so read and take note...

THE HOURS: Breakfast will be served between 7.30 and 8.30, which are the most cruelly inappropriate hours for any idler. The B&B owners clearly choose them to ensure you're in such a rush when you get up that you've no time to use your complimentary sachets of tea and coffee. Remember: the miniature kettle and out-of-date Millac Maids are for ornamental purposes only. Leave them on the doyley where they belong. Shake your lover from their blessed slumber and stumble downstairs to face your fate. Cursing under your breath is acceptable.

THE BREAKFAST ROOM: It will be too small, with too many tables, set too close together. You enter at 8.29, feeling and looking like shit, and all the other guests will be there before you. The pictures by local artists on the walls and the plastic flowers at the tables will not hide the fact that you are sat in the corner of a strange couple's living room. It is the done thing to pretend, like everyone else, that this is completely normal.

THE OTHER GUESTS: Everyone will look embarrassed by the enforced intimacy of the situation. They'll try and alleviate the discomfort by greeting you in an overly friendly way. You are not required to ask if they slept well, but you will be expected to catch eyes with one person at each table in turn, giving them a short and confident "good morning".

THE VOLUME: You have already made the loudest utterance that is acceptable throughout the breakfast sitting. From now on, all conversation must be conducted at a at a barely-audible level. This convention has arisen from the fact that none of the other guests are in the slightest bit interested in what each other has to say. They've lowered their voices in the hope of catching a snippet from the people sat next to them. But their neighbours, in turn, are doing exactly the same. A descending spiral of soft-speaking ensues. You and your partner might feel an overwhelming urge to shout obscenities at the top of your voice. It is known as 'B&B Tourette's' and must be resisted at all costs.

THE OWNERS: Your breakfast will be prepared and served by Mr and Mrs Weird. There will be something creepy about them. He'll be sycophantic and overly-interested in his guests' private lives. She'll be so sick of strangers cluttering her house that she'll hate the very sight of you. Interaction with both should be kept to a minimum. It's easily done in her case. But he is armed with a social tractor

MORNING!

beam. Don't get caught in it. The following topics spell danger: how long the two of you have been together, whether your bed springs were too noisy and whether you'd like him to show you a trick to make the shower work better. Order your breakfast with single-word sentences and keep eye contact to a minimum.

THE DRINKS: The orange juice will have been watered down to make twice as much. This age-old B&B tradition leaves you with a dilemma: avoid it completely, as it tastes so insipid, or drink twice as much to get a normal glass-worth. Either way, it is the done thing to refer to the tea and coffee as "hot beverages".

THE FOOD: It is tempting to pretend that the mini cartons of cereal are in fact normal-size and that the two of you have woken up as giants. This is not to be done. It is also bad form to be picky with the fried breakfast, as the owners will consider each item refused as an incremental slight. It is, however, acceptable to leave the triangles of cold toast in the rack. They will appreciate being able to re-serve them for the following morning. ◉

THE GOOD LIFE:
LOOK AFTER YOURSELF

The great self-sufficiency pioneer John Seymour died this year.
But his work is being carried forward by William Sutherland,
who runs courses at their Irish smallholding

Our successful students call themselves "DFKs" (Debt Free Killers) whilst an American marketing guru would probably call us "a kinda midwife of transition between the rat race and the good life". Puzzled? Well it gets worse when we start talking about the "merchants of greed" and their "poodle faker" acolytes. Of course we grow our own food too, build our own homes, drink our own beer, cure our own bacon and make our own music.

So what exactly is the School for Self Sufficiency – where are we, what do we do and how did it all start? The School was created by John Seymour and Angela Ashe in 1992. Its syllabus is *The New Complete Book of Self Sufficiency* which was originally conceived in the 1970s by John Seymour and became the best selling foundation for the Dorling Kindersley publishing empire. Its students are mostly successful professionals or well educated young graduates who have growing doubts about continuing their careers in the cut and thrust of modern business life.

We do our living and teaching in a beautifully secluded smallholding at Killowen on the banks of the great river Barrow in the Republic of Ireland. Around us are huge beech trees and below us is the sparkling river. Our animals and plants live with us too and we have a constant stream of students and visitors sitting at our table.

Sometimes it is difficult to decide whether we are eco-warriors, lifestyle gurus, eccentric performance artists or mere creatures of the soil – soil organisms in fact. Perhaps we are all of these things! Suffice to say life is very seldom dull. The smallholding is its own small world of animals, plants, pests and disease and we humans use all the cunning we can muster to persuade nature to be both bountiful and benign.

Let me retrace my steps briefly to revisit the poodle fakers and Debt Free Killers. Seymour's views on the urban rich are neatly contained in his term "poodle faker"? A poodle is a fancy overbred dog which has no practical value other than show. A faker is a worthless person whose life is one of pretence. Put the two together and you get the picture. DFK, on the other hand, came from one of our earliest students and was a bit of a surprise as we had not realised how our teachings might affect people. We first met George when he came down from his city accounting job to have few days exposure to our way of life. Some years later he had sold up in the city, wiped out his debt and brought his wife and family down to a pleasant 20 acre farm just a few miles away. After he had had 12 months of his new life to contend with I asked him how he felt his life had changed. He said that there had been two major

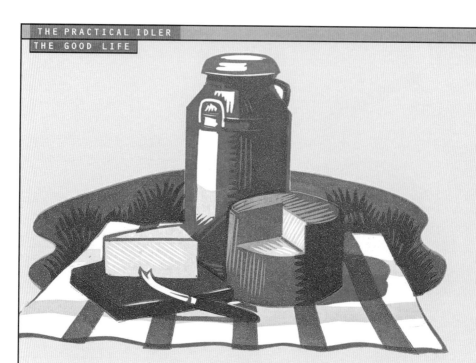

changes – on the one hand he now had no debts to worry about and on the other he found himself continually killing things either to stop them eating his vegetables or in order to eat them himself. Neither of these things had he really expected. When I thought about it I suppose city people take the existence of debt as a fact of life just as country people understand that killing things is a necessary part of being one of the humans on planet Earth.

And what about the vegetarians? Well, we have plenty of those who visit us too. Most have very worthy and sensible reasons for their choice but few understand the mechanics of real life. Take the simple case of the cow for example. To get milk from this cow you need to produce one calf each year (cows make milk to feed the calves which humans then remove to "steal" the milk). Half of these calves are female and will themselves go on to produce one calf each year unless some kind of forcible birth control intervenes. At this rate the exponential growth of the cow population over say 25 years (a reasonable life span for a cow) would produce over one million beasts without human intervention! I suppose wolves or lions could be used for control but that might bring its own ethical problems. The moral of this is that if we have these animals at all then we have to manage them and do it as humanely and wisely as we can.

And let's not forget our fellow humans who we call the "merchants of greed". Basically these are the folk flying round in helicopters and big cars. Mostly they are creatures of big corporations; they mine the planet and its people for their own ends. In practice they don't have the time to enjoy themselves until they retire and then it is too late – first they have forgotten how and second they are probably too overweight and riddled with cancer and ulcers anyway. The secret of their power lies in an extraordinary skill in selling people things they do not really need.

Enough of the preaching. What sort of fellow was this John Seymour who just died at the age of 90 years? In his own words, he was a man who "lived and loved both well and dangerously." His early dream was to be a cowboy and as soon as his schooling at Wye Agricultural college was complete he set off for Africa where he worked as veterinary officer, copper miner, and fishing boat captain. After fighting through the gruelling Burma campaign during the Second World War he lived for a time in a converted trolley bus, worked coastal sailing ships and began to write. He became a popular broadcaster with the BBC and made some of the very first environmental films in the 1970s. His wide knowledge came from his passion for reading and his easy conversational writing was always full of amusing human anecdotes. John saw in his work and travels how neither wealth, nor the flash of Hollywood glamour could bring happiness. He believed that we should cut out what we do not need so we can live more simply and happily. Good food, comfortable clothes, serviceable hous-

ing and true culture – those are the things Seymour believed really mattered.

As for myself, well I was the son of a traditional farmer who made it to work at the centre of things as a management consultant in the big city. What I discovered there changed my views. When I met John in 1991 I liked his work and decided I would try to keep it going by helping him found the School of Self Sufficiency with Angela. Little did I realise how my life would change and here I am 12 years later, married to Angela and sitting writing at our sturdy beech coffee table. I made this table from the trunk of the beech tree which John and Angela cut down from the front of the house when they first came here.

The *New Complete Book* continues to sell in book-

shops around the world. The garden is better than ever and a new generation of bouncy pigs graces the old sty. My two youngest children beaver away, harvesting and playing in the garden. Chickens scratch away in the orchard and beside them the latest crop of delicious horse mushrooms has just been fried up for my breakfast. Right now my time is spent dealing with several hundredweight of apples (cider, apple pulp, and apple jelly), as well as harvesting and processing the year's carrot crop and pickling the beetroot. We have a young German teacher from the Black Forest helping us at the moment and a Frenchman is on his way by bicycle from the west coast. Life goes on and there should be a good session at the village pub tonight. ☺

JOHN SEYMOUR
The NEW
complete book *of*
SELF-
SUFFICIENCY
—— The classic guide ——
for realists and dreamers

Here is the new edition of John Seymour's classic. Or look for the old one on abebooks.com

IDLE PURSUITS:
THE URBAN BEEKEEPER

Beehive yourself, says Chris Draper

Recently eating a piece of toast I noticed once again, something that I had forgotten since childhood: the darkly sinister labelling of Golden Syrup. An ingenious reference to honey is made via the morbid image of a cloud of bees flying out of the corpse of a dead lion over the byline "out of the strong came forth sweetness", presumably a biblical reference to Samson's story, also a veiled reference to Mr Tate's colonial leanings, given that his amber syrup relied on human labour rather than that of *Apis Melifera*, the European Honeybee.

Traditionally the domain of the briar-smoking bachelor curate, or the non-communicative pastoral type wth trousers held up with baling twine, beekeeping is undergoing a new renaissance. It's never going to be the new rock and roll but a cross between skiffle and Nick Drake is a good place to find yourself.

If you've ever given any thought to honey and beehives, images of apple orchards, rolling fields or village vicarage gardens often spring to mind but according to the latest figures there are nearly three thousand urban beekeepers within the M25 and the numbers are growing each year. Many beekeepers both

PROFESSOR RILEY, CURATOR OF INSECTS. 1843–1895

rural and urban retired as a result of the devastating Varroa Destructor mite which wiped out thousands of colonies when it arrived in the UK in 1992, but with new approaches and adaptations a new generation of beekeepers are discovering the fascination and benefits of keeping a couple of hives at the end of the garden or in their allotment (some even keeping them on the balconies of their flats or on flat rooves).

My own experience started last year, when John Chapple, South London's swarm collector, arrived

early one Saturday morning in May with two ominously humming boxes, which he placed on the kitchen floor. The previous January I had enrolled on a beekeeping course at Roots and Shoots, a community garden in Lambeth, along with about twenty others of mixed ages, backgrounds and a fairly even split of the sexes. Every Thursday evening we would meet for theory, anatomical and practical demonstrations of the dark arts. As a collector of trivia, these evenings provided a rich source of pickings: "It takes two million flowers to make a pound of honey", "Two out of every three mouthfuls of food we eat are pollinated by bees", "Bees can fly seven million miles to the gallon (of honey)" are some of the more memorable. Throughout the winter I consumed every book on the subject I could lay my hands on and became increasingly impatient. Now all that theory and dreaming were about to be put into practice, with the aid of about 40,000 bees. Theory is one thing but it's not until you are surrounded by a cloud of disorientated and angry bees that you realise whether you are cut out for this or not. Technically you could learn most of the basics from a book, but this is why I would recommend anyone considering keeping bees to enrol on a practical course, or work with an experienced beekeeper for a while. Tools of the trade are pretty basic: a veil to keep bees out of your eyes and mouth, a smoker to calm the bees, a hive tool and obviously a hive or two. Beekeeping is not for the fashionably faint hearted. Black veils, leather gauntlets and broad brimmed hats are only for the most adventurous or those who use specialised pay-per-view websites. Unannounced trips to the hives can lead to neighbours assuming you are running your own WMD programme (firing beehives at the enemy as in the siege of Chester, 908 AD must count as the

It takes two million flowers to make a pound of honey. Two out of every three mouthfuls of food we eat are pollinated by bees

earliest example of bio-warfare).

Hives come in different shapes and sizes, all having their benefits and drawbacks, fans and detractors. Whatever you choose, a hive is basically a convenient, accessible, simulation of a hollow tree, which is where wild bees would naturally build their colonies. As a beekeeper, you can't domesticate bees. They are still essentially wild, but you try and work with their natural instincts as opposed to fighting them. It's pretty obvious who's going to come off worse if you go down that route.

The generosity of more experienced keepers constantly amazed me, given the dog eat dog world of South West London. Generous with time, advice, and in my case the inheritance of two hives from a retiring keeper in Wimbledon, which were then lovingly burnt out with a flame-torch to kill any lurking diseases. Unfortunately, the hives contained no bees, the colonies having died out over a series of bad winters. A site where flying bees wouldn't disturb the neighbours was chosen and the hives reassembled. On a slightly cool and damp Saturday morning and under John's patient eye we took the boxes to the end of the garden and emptied the swarms into their new homes. After a quick cup of coffee, he jumped into his van and sped off to another collection, leaving me elated, nervous and with a strangely pleasant sense of responsibility. I wandered through the drizzle back up to the hives to check the bees were still resident.

In short, the hive consists of a brood chamber (where the eggs are laid and young reared), supers (where honey is stored) and a roof. A metal grill (the queen excluder) prevents the queen laying eggs in the honey supers. Each hive contains one queen, workers (up to 60,000 at the height of the season) and some drones. All the workers are female, the drones being supported in the hive for breeding purposes, though if they are still there at the end of the season they will be thrown out of the hives by the workers. So much for progressive societies. Ironically the symbol of the beehive has been used in both left and right wing propaganda in various parts of the world and at various times. It has been presented as both the perfect monarchist state and the perfect social collective, sometimes at the same time.

The first thing that surprised me was how small honeybees are. In my biological naivety I had visions of bumblebee style insects. Food packaging images, in this case honey, have a lot to answer for when it comes to townies' views of nature. The bees are actually little larger than houseflies, and depending on the strain of bee can range from black, grey to brown. No discernible smiling face or shiny pointy sting can be made out by the naked eye.

Once settled in, maintenance is low, but regularity is important. Preventing bees' natural instinct to

swarm is one reason; monitoring for diseases is another. These include such fascinating sounding things as American Foul Brood, European Foul Brood, Chalk Brood and Varroa Destructor, all of which would make potentially interesting film titles. Unchecked, any of these could wipe out both your colonies and those of other local keepers, so there's a strong element of responsibility in ensuring that these don't go undiagnosed.

Last Autumn we had our first, aromatic crop of Streatham honey. Thick, delicious, dripping from the honeycomb into a tray on the kitchen table, filling the whole house with the heavy scent of the summer that had just passed. That's Christmas presents and birthday presents sorted out for a while as well as the house consumption of honey.

I'm writing this in the early summer and though the honey crop won't be ready to be taken off the hives for a few more months, I am plotting methods, as Marx would say, "of alienating the workers from the fruits of their production." 🐝

BECOME A BEEKEEPER
Roots and Shoots will be running evening courses on Beekeeping from January 2005. Those interested should contact David Perkins on 020 7587 1131 or contact their local branch of the British Beekeepers Association

LINDA SCOTT

IDLE PUSUITS
DELICIOUS CREAM TEAS

Sarah Janes remembers the good times and the bad

Most hardcore cream tea enthusiasts will be reading this from heaven because there's only so much artery clogging, blood-clotting clotted cream a chap or chapess can devour before it's time to say hello to that benevolent bearded breadmaker in the sky. But I am young and rosy-cheeked with plenty of healthy ventricles left to fur up. Still, if my lust for scones and cream and strawberry jam do land me in an early grave, so be it. At least I will die happy, although I will probably be in a considerable amount of pain.

I'm a strong believer that food should be made with love and care, lots of it. It

You are a fat, furry, beautiful bumblebee, gorged on the blood of an orchid, drowning in honey, bee-leg in bee-leg with your buzzing beloved

tastes better, it makes you feel good. This is particularly true of a cream tea. Like drunken sex, unless you do it with someone you love, you will probably wish you hadn't. Shortly afterwards you might feel guilty and a little sick, oh and dirty and sort of ugly. Whereas with love in the scone-jam-cream equation, you are a fat, furry, beautiful bumblebee, gorged on the blood of an orchid, drowning in honey, beeleg in beeleg with your buzzing beloved, in a gentle breeze in a soft, sweet, poppy-sprinkled meadow at sunset.

The Mock Turtle (Pool Valley, Brighton) is the most delicious cream tea establishment I have ever been to, and I pride myself on having been to more cream tea establishments than the average mortal. They make a perfect scone and they always arrive warm and flour-dusted. Cups and saucers of the blue and white and chipped variety prevail, as do sugar tongs, loose leaf tea blends, ancient tea pots and Alice in Wonderland Victoriana. Certain old dears are in there eating kippers every day and menus are hand-written with italic flourishes. Little love notes and the poems of patrons written on grease-spotted doilies line the drawers of old tables. It is a mainstay of locals and an irresistible olde worlde jam-trap for tourists and is thronging with the latter at the weekends. It is nicest on a weekday when it's black and grey and pissing down outside.

There's also a great little place overlooking Mortehoe graveyard near Woolacoombe in Devon, which is like having a cream tea in someone's proper old nan's living room. Me and my bestest pal went there once and afterwards we collected marbles from the beach and she sat on the cliff edge whilst I threw little dried bits of sheep whoopsy in her general direction and she held her mouth open and I said if I got one in she had to eat it and she agreed. Luckily for her I'm left-, or in Nanspeak, cack-handed, and throwing was never my forte. That was a fine, fine day.

Another fine cream tea day was years ago, another one in Devon or maybe Cornwall. Ma and Pa Janes had just had a blazing row because Ma Janes bought Pa Janes a mug what said – "PRE-

SENTED TO THE WORLD'S BIGGEST BAS-
TARD". Despite nearly cracking the
offending item against the "foul-mouthed
old trollop's" forehead at the time, Pa
Janes still enjoys the mammoth cuppa it
can contain every now and again, it's
writing somewhat faded but still pertinent.

Anywhose, on the day in question, the
whole Janes posse boarded a little boat
which took us to a thatched cottage on
its own island and we saw a seal. In the
thatched cottage we had a cream tea.
The silky, buttery texture of the clotted
cream (slut and queen of the cream
world), the sweet, saliva inducing proper-
ties of the homemade strawberry jam
and the floury cumulus quality of the
scone escape me but we saw a seal and
Ma and Pa stewed longer than the tea.

More recently I rushed home from the
Janes Family Homestead to enjoy a Mock
Turtle cream tea with my friend
Scabbers. I was in such a hurry that I forgot to buy a ticket for the train and was
read my rights by rail cops at the
Brighton barriers. I says, "Look here, I
don't mean to be rude but I have rather
an urgent cream tea to attend to. I'm
expected." They said, "What's your name
and address?" I told them, they called
someone who might have been sitting in
front of a phone book, then they said,
"You don't live there," and I said, "Yes, I do"
and they said, "All right, then".

I was quizzed as to my fare-evading
intentions. The bad rail cop said, "I propose you didn't intend to pay for a ticket",
I says, "You're quite right". The good rail
copette says, "Check this statement that
I've written down and sign here". The bad
rail cop softened and the good rail
copette says, "Description... hmmm." I
struck what I thought was a rather hilarious Freemans catalogue type slack pose,

someone said "gorgeous". Bad rail cop
said, "About 20." I says, "27, actually".
Copette said, "I would have said 20, too." I
laughed, acted a-blush. Really bad,
naughty rail cop says "Single?" I says, "as
it happens." He says, "Doing anything
tonight?" I says, "Not with you". Whole
thing deteriorated into giggles. A series of
little train-driving dwarfs were brought in
to work out how tall I was. I says: "I don't
know about fining me, I'll have you for
sexual harassment or something". He
says: "I don't care, I'm leaving next week."

Was less than 10 minutes late for
Scabbers and also had rather amusing
anecdote for him what made the afternoon all the more strawberry sweet. We
read each other's tea leaves. The Mock
Turtle is a leaves and strainer affair
which makes amateur tea-leaf reading
possible. Cream tea is also brilliant
because it provides a sense of occasion
for cracking an excellent joke I heard on
Southern Counties radio last night to
whomsoever is being "Mother". "How do
you like your tea, darling?" "I like my tea
like my men... weak." Ha, hahahahahahaha-
ha!

Ah, so many cream teas, so many
memories! ☺

THE BROWSER:
A BOOKSHOP OF NOTE

Jock Scot visits Denis Rixon's "Midge Repellent Portakabin Bookshop", Mallaig, Scotland

Most visitors to the Isle of Skye who do not drive or sail there, will take the train from Glasgow Queen Street via Rannoch Moor to Mallaig on the West Highland Line. One of Europe's most enjoyable train journeys, certainly the most romantic, and, with a five hour duration, one of the best for getting tipsy on.

Lean back in your pre-booked window seat, fac-ing the direction of travel, and get outside of a bottle of your favourite whiskey (Irn-Bru mixer optional). Let the train take the strain, relax and say "Hi-yah!" to your brain and remind yourself that your mouth is a drain.

The West Highland Line is the

A GUID PLACE TAE CRASH IF...

jewel in the crown of the Scottish Crown Jewels of travel, and can get busy for no obvious reason. Frequented by outward-bound Monroe-baggers and, increasingly, by Harry Potter fanatics, as a section of the line with viaduct-style bridge was featured in the movie.

On school holidays it can be crammed with JK Rowling readers as they head for "Harry Potter Land."

When you alight at the terminus of Mallaig, where ferries serve Skye, Jura, Eigg, Muck and the Small Isles of the Utter Hebrides, find time to drop in on Denis Rixson's "Midge Repellant Portakabin Bookshop."

Directions: exit station, take a right past the fresh fish and kipper shop, past the Marine Bar and Bank, next right and there you are, on the right at the fit o' the brae that runs up and away frae the her–burr opposite the Steam Inn, just by the wheelie-bin (see photo).

Here you can stock up on essentials before boarding ferry or boat to mainland UK's remotest pub, midge rep, maps, postcards, bagpipe music on C.D. Punk rock, pink fishing nets for t'weans etc, etc. But most thrillingly he has a really eclectic selection of wonderful books on Scots subjects (sorry it has taken 400 words to get you in the door, but it really is a trip of a trip). If you arrive after four in the evening or at the weekend the proprietor may be in, checking the till roll and so on. Author of definitive books on History of Local Area, Dennis also teaches at the local school and looks after his two kids. ◉

THE BROWSER:
PLAY IT, FUCKING LOUD

The *Idler* was in Manchester and the sun was out which gives Manchester a kind of Manhattan vibe, so we popped in to the Cornerhouse Bookshop to see what they're reading

Tim is the shop manager and he showed us round. "Because Cornerhouse is also a venue, with a cinema and exhibitions, our stock is predominantly magazines and cinema books: everything from the new Kieslowski (Between Theory and Post-theory) to Russ Meyer. The BFI Modern Classics series are great. We have all of them – they're very popular. There's Iain Sinclair on Cronenberg and Ballard's *Crash*, of course, among the newest ones in the series are books on *Withnail and I* and *Nosferatu*. We also sell a lot of art books, and in fact Cornerhouse are an art books distributor – probably the biggest in the

country, you should check out our website, there's some great stuff... a lot of people come to Manchester because of the city's music culture and one of my favourite books about this is *Shake Rattle and Rain*, by CP Lee, which is a book about every band that ever played in Manchester. CP Lee used to sing with Alberto y Los Trios Paranoias: not quite as famous as John the Postman, in

ly, documented as the "Albert Hall Bootleg", this was the moment when Dylan alienated his massive, folky fan base in the UK by playing out and out rock and roll, with electric guitars and everything. Lee points out that until this moment even the biggest bands toured with relatively low-level amplification – just a bunch of little amps rather than a sound system, but that's what Dylan had, and as a result this gig was probably the loudest thing anybody in the audience had ever heard in their lives. Lee is great on the strictures of the very right-on Manchester Folk scene, which was militantly prescriptive about what songs could or should be about. At least it was until this gig. At one point, as is well known, an irate folky shouts "Judas!" – giving a voice to the audience members who until that point had contented themseves with slow-handclapping and walking out to signal the collective sense of betrayal. Interrupted while introducing the next song, Dylan's response is to instruct the band to "Play it fucking loud!"

Manchester terms, but they're legendary... kind of snuff rock. I'm pretty sure he used to hang himself on stage. Actually I think he might be in the bar if you want to meet him."

Tim's a good salesman. CP Lee wasn't in the bar, but I did buy a copy of *Shake Rattle and Rain* to read on the train. It's a great little book, a series of essays that pick up the history of popular music in Manchester, from the jazz and folk eras right through the Sex Pistols gig at the Lesser Free Trade Hall to Madchester and beyond. It's full of interviews, rumours and gossip.

Amongst the inevitable Tony Wilson interviews there are discussions of the fanzine scene. One of the most interesting chapters concerns itself with a legendary Bob Dylan gig – also at the Free Trade Hall – but ten years before the Sex Pistols (though it seems to belong to a different age altogether). A concert most famously, and wrong-

Lee's book is scatty and inspiring enough to have me seeking out the recent CBS re-release of this Dylan bootleg and a cheap copy of *Never Mind the Bollocks*, and it makes a great companion volume to Jeff Noon's brilliant dub-skiffle novel *Needle in the Groove*, Nicholas Blincoe's *Manchester Slingback*, Dave Haslam's *Manchester, England* and Simon Ford's *Mark E. Smith* and The Fall biog *Hip Priest*. Which should keep you going you can next pop into Cornerhouse. ☺

CP Lee, Shake Rattle and Rain: Popular Music Making in Manchester 1955-1995, *Hardinge Simpole*, £15.00 • *Kevin Jackson*, Withnail and I, *BFI Modern Classics*, £8.99 • *S.S.Prawer*, Nosferatu: Phantom der Nacht, *BFI Modern Classics*, £8.99
http://www.cornerhouse.org/publications/

BOOKS:
THE HEDONISM HANDBOOK

By Michael Flocker (Da Capo Press, 2004)

Hedonism, like idleness, has become a sadly neglected way of life. Living in a world obsessed with work and money, insane diets and inane celebrities, it's become clear to American author Michael Flocker that somewhere along the way we've forgotten how to have a good time. For many, hedonism has become a bad thing, a dirty word associated with debauched Roman orgies or Essex lads excessing in Eyebeefa. But this is not what hedonism is about. Flocker stresses the need for a restrained form of pleasure. The consequences of our actions must always be considered; balance is the key. The road of excess does not lead to the palace of wisdom, it leads to a bloody big hangover.

The author certainly possesses a good old-fashioned notion of hedonism: he provides an entertaining history, recounting the stories of infamous nutcases like Caligula (the one who made his horse a consul) and King Ludwig (the one who built the Chitty Chitty Bang Bang castle); he delves into those mainstays of the hedonistic lifestyle - drink, drugs, food and sex; and in a chapter entitled 'Beautiful Things' he states that "Camels and peacocks can really add drama to an otherwise uninspired garden."

But Flocker wants us to look closely at our lives, and he repeatedly reassures us that it's never too late to change our ways. We must get rid of our crazy ambitions to get to the finish line first, to achieve celebrity status, to get stick-thin, to land that lucrative contract. We must be ourselves; we must not care what society thinks of success or beauty. We must, as the scholar, writer and teacher Joseph Campbell said, "Follow our bliss."

Whilst Flocker's subject is timeless, this book is concerned with the now. In this hyperkinetic age "the intoxicating state we seek is no longer that of the drug-induced stupor, but rather a complete and utter lack of stimulation."

Modern hedonism therefore becomes a reaction against the modern world. "Just a few stolen moments away from the television, computer screens, traffic, politics, showbusiness, advertising, neon lights and continuous noise has become either a distant memory or a distant dream of some future escape to a tropical island." What we really need is "silence, stillness and tranquility... luxuries available to all, regardless of budget."

The Hedonism Handbook is an extremely wise book, vividly written with bone-dry wit, and beautifully illustrated in decadent red and black – it is, in short, a genuine pleasure. ☻

EDWARD SAGE

HOW
TO
BE LAZY
HEALTHY
&
FiT

by Peter J. Steincrohn, M.D.

A WINNING
TITLE AND A
LOVELY BOOK,
FROM 1968

USEFUL BOOKS:

Doctors prove that doing nothing is good for your health

The idea that idleness is good for you enjoyed a brief vogue in the late sixties with fantastic titles in the US such as the one above. Now the ideas are back: next year sees the publication of *The Joy of* *Laziness: How To Slow Down And Live Longer* (Bloomsbury) by Germans Dr Peter Axt and Dr Michaela Axt-Gaderman. It counsels against the gym and argues that "late sleepers live longer."

THE BOOKSHELF OF
GEORGE SHAW

These bookshelves belong to the artist George Shaw. George is most celebrated for his photo-realist paintings of deserted scenes from the council estate in Coventry where he grew up. His books *This Was LIfe* and *What I Did This Summer* (Ikon Gallery) are available for £5.95 and £14.95 respectively, from Amazon.

LOVE MUSIC HATE RACISM, 16 MARCH 2004

EASY SOUNDS:
PETER DOHERTY

Edward Sage on the ex-Libertine turned Babyshambles
frontman. Photographs by Andrew Kendall

It's a sad fact that many people will have been introduced to The Libertines because of Peter Doherty's well-publicized private life, specifically his addiction to heroin and crack cocaine. Countless newspaper articles about his failed visits to rehab appeared over the summer. "Annihilation beckons the dark star of rock," read the *Observer*'s headline. "He will die like his hero Vicious," read the *Sun*'s. Doherty was compared to both Sid Vicious and Kurt Cobain in these pieces, and if you believe what you read, he's seemingly on a mission to join the "stupid club" that Cobain's mother spoke of; but these comparisons are pertinent also because Pete is, like Sid and Kurt, the icon of the most important musical movement of his generation.

There have been so many twists and turns and ups and downs in the short history of The Libertines that it sometimes feels unreal - like a lurid rock 'n' roll movie is being played out before your eyes. Their story has been well-documented now, but for those unfamiliar, here is a brief synopsis of the plot so far: in the late nineties Peter Doherty meets Carl Barat in London; they become best friends and form The Libertines, sharing singing, songwriting and guitar-playing duties. John Hassall is recruited on bass and Gary Powell becomes drummer. They are signed by Rough Trade, record an album called *Up The Bracket* in the summer of 2002, and embark on a UK tour which the NME later describes as "one of the most debauched tours in recent rock history". In February 2003 The Libertines are named Best New Band at the NME Awards. In June, however, Doherty refuses to go on their European tour – he feels slighted after Barat fails to turn up to one of their "secret" gigs. When the band returns Doherty is sacked and he forms a side project named Babyshambles. While The Libertines play a concert in Japan, Doherty is arrested for burgling Barat's flat. A few weeks after becoming a father he admits to a newspaper that he's addicted to heroin and crack. On 8 September 2003 24-year-old Doherty is sentenced to six months in prison - he serves half of a reduced sentence of two months. On the day of his release Barat meets him at the prison gates and they travel to Kent where they play an emotional reunion gig in a pub in front of 200 fans (the Freedom Gig is named the top live moment in 2003 by the NME). Shortly afterwards, Alan McGee becomes their manager. In February 2004 The Libertines win Best British Band at the NME Awards. They record their second album, simply titled *The Libertines*. Doherty goes on a UK tour with Babyshambles. There is a riot at a gig in Stoke and part of the venue collapses. The venue's promoters book them again for the following week. Still addicted to the Class A's, Pete begins a series of unsuccessful stints in rehab, first at the Priory and then at a monastery in Thailand. He leaves the monastery after a few days, travels to Bangkok and scores drugs, flies back to London and is promptly arrested for possession of a flick knife. Doherty is sacked from the band again until he kicks the drugs. In August he is attacked in Farringdon and gets hit by a car whilst trying to

BRING ME MY BOW OF BURNING GOLD, BRING ME MY ARROWS OF DESIRE

escape. On 1 September he is driven to court; he is standing up through the sun-roof singing and playing guitar. He receives a four month suspended sentence. At the end of September he fails to perform at a Babyshambles gig in Aberdeen; the audience is told he fell down the steps of his tour bus; fans riot and seven people are arrested.

It's an incredible story but it would be a pity if the soap-opera overshadowed the music. The Libertines are a punk band, but they possess a rare ability to weave Beatles-like pop melodies into that ragged punk rock noise. The guitars are jangling, raucous, seemingly out of control, perfect. Doherty / Barat lyrics are beautifully poetic and wonderfully witty. They veer from the sublime ("If you've lost your faith in love and music/The end won't be long") to the sublimely ridiculous ("What a divvy, what a fucking div/talking like a moron, walking like a spiv"). They sing about class

("You come up the hard way, they remind you every day/You're nothing") and poverty ("Got matches & cable TV, half of less than 50p"), and love and friendship – the second album tells the tale of the fragile relationship between the two frontmen. Their vision of England encompasses the harsh reality of riots and street violence, dole queues, booze and drugs, racism, cheap hotels and lonely streets; but they also possess a charming notion of an old-world or idyllic Albion evoked with images of pith helmets, spies in trees, gin in tea cups and leaves on the lawn. They can be angry and sarcastic but they're never morose. They are also notably unsentimental. In "The Good Old Days" they declare: "It chars my heart to always hear you calling/Calling for the good old days/Because there were no 'good old days'/These are the good old days." They also have a wonderful way with swear words: their debut single "What A Waster" was banned on Radio 1 due to its numerous fucks, pisses and cunts; and anyone who has witnessed the crowd singing along during a live performance of "I Get Along" will agree that they can be credited with inventing the most cathartic use of the word fuck in the history of music: "I get along just singing my song/People tell me I'm wrong/Fuck 'em!"

When Carl Barat was asked who or what inspires him, he said: "Sid James and Sid Vicious". His quip is interesting because The Libertines do seem to embody a similarly diverse yet quintessentially English image – they're both lovable rogues and snarling punk rock troubadours, Terry-Thomas meets Joe Strummer. They wear suits, trilbies, brown brogues, cravats, braces, scarlet guardsmen's tunics, ripped jeans and leather jackets. In interviews they attempt morris-dancing and sing music hall songs. Doherty has even constructed a mythical English world for himself and the band to inhabit; a world where England is seen as the good ship Albion sailing the stormy seas, onwards to happy times in Arcadia – an imagined realm of the infinite, a place "where cigarettes grow on trees and all the benches are made of denim". Pete's personal philosophy is that the purpose of life is to reach this fabled place. "I've believed in it since I was 15," said Pete. "When I first met Carl and told him of Arcadia, he believed me."

Their other philosophy is to live their lives as libertines, free from moral restraint and the constrictions imposed by modern society.

Doherty in particular appears to do whatever the fuck he wants. When he actually turns up to a gig, he is as capricious onstage as he is off it. I've seen him hurl his guitar into the audience halfway through a song; smash his vintage Rickenbacker after a just a few songs; incite stage invasions and pull fans past incredulous security. Pete and Carl have even had fights on stage. At a gig in Leeds in 2002 Doherty attempted to grab a badge from Carl's back to throw into the crowd. Carl turned round and hit him in the face with his guitar. "He was so deranged and hyped up on stage that even me putting my hand on his shoulder was too much," said Pete. Alan McGee has said that The Libertines are more difficult to manage than Oasis.

Doherty has always strived to be accessible to his fans. Pete bares his heart and soul on babyshambles.com and often chats to fans on the libertines.org forum. After a session in the Chelsea Hotel in New York in which they laid down

BACKSTAGE AT A BABYSHAMBLES GIG IN LONDON, 6 OCTOBER 2004

SUNDAY NIGHT AT PETE'S, 18 JANUARY 2004

more than forty tracks, they gave the recording to a fan in the lobby. In early March The Libertines played three consecutive nights at the Brixton Academy. At the last gig Pete smashed his guitar halfway through the set and stormed off stage. His bandmates stopped playing, exited briefly, and then returned as a three-piece with John singing back-up vocals. When Pete came back on a few songs later, his chest gashed, he apologised to the crowd, saying: "Sorry about that. I had a bit of a strop." On 12 March Pete celebrated his twenty-fifth birthday; a couple of days later he posted this message on the band's website: "Timeless boohooing about Biggles [Carl] not being my mate. Never does 'owt to reach out to me, loves me but doesn't like me. No birthday pressie or even message or anything since I left dressing room at Brixton on Sunday. But this is normal and so why now let it upset me... The one true horror is that if I was to be true to myself as an artist, as a man, as a libertine, I would not work with the band as it stands anymore. The release and liberty of the other path, ie, Babyshambles, Peter Doherty solo or whatever is immense I can feel it from this side like barbed wire, like in the cell in Wanno [Wandsworth] last year. Like a weight off me poor bony old shoulders... I need to speak to the boys before I go nuts. Maybe I don't know what I'm talking about. Maybe they know how I feel but are holding out at whatever cost. We have a good thing going etc etc, but fuck em, he's a difficult man to love and he gives me nothing. I go through each day and am twisting up, when I finally, fully unwind it will be furious, disastrous, dangerous, spectacular."

The Libertines have played many secret gigs, or guerilla gigs as they've become known. These shows are announced to the public usually on Doherty's website, and often on the same day of the performance. Pubs in North London or the East End are typical venues. A few days after the Freedom Gig they played two shows in one afternoon in Regents Park, first in the bandstand, and second on a small island in the middle of the lake. Shortly after a gig at the Duke of Clarence in February, McGee said: "Give us a venue and we'll give you a show. That's why we're doing this, to remind people what rock 'n' roll is about." And when they can't get a venue they play gigs in Pete's flat. Below is an example of a secret gig with three performances announced via Doherty's website:

£10 entry to Albion rooms to see the pair of us performing our favourite songs from the vaults and the newly blossoming branches of arcady.

First sitting will be gathered lovingly by a Libertine in a hat at Whitechapel underground's photobooth..

12.00pm sharp for 12.30pm performance.

No liggers. Instruments welcomed, and a bit of what you fancy.

Evening shows 10.30pm start (tickets to be presented by ourselves in person at 10.15pm, outside or inside Blind Beggar)

second evening show 11.30pm start (tickets on the door, 18 collingwood house, Darling Row E1)

Carlos & Peter x

On this particular evening the gig was cancelled at the last minute ("due to heartbreak") but it was still an enjoyable evening. In fact, I first met Tom, the editor of the magazine you are holding, in the Blind Beggar that evening. Although bands have been playing secret gigs for years, the Libertines have seemingly reinvented this phenomenon and made it their own; they've created a little subculture where people with a common interest in music can meet and become friends. At the beginning of August I went to a flat gig with Dan, the *Idler*'s Deputy Editor. The message on the website promised "lunch and fine wines". When we

"I think I belong to a community, which I'm pretty sure the boss of Time Warner isn't in"

got there Peter offered us Haribo bears and Special Brew and then played an amazing hour-long solo acoustic set.

Peter and The Libertines have managed to rejuvenate the London rock scene by instilling a DIY ethic similar to that of the seventies punk movement. They have inspired people to form bands and have invited smaller groups like The Others, Thee Unstrung, The Paddingtons and Special Needs to perform with them at club nights like 'Bring Your Own Poison' at Whitechapel's Rhythm Factory – the Roxy or CBGBs of this second punk movement. This generation, however, is blessed with new technology like the internet and mobile phones. You can post on Network 54 forums and talk to like-minded music fans; you can find out about guerilla gigs just hours before they take place; and you can download MP3s and amateur videos of gigs for free. Right now there is the feeling that rock 'n' roll is being dragged away from the music industry. Kids are scrawling the slogans of their beloved bands on the

THE STROKES
Room On Fire
CD/vinyl LP

THE LIBERTINES
The Libertines
CD/Ltd. heavy vinyl LP

BELLE AND SEBASTIAN
Dear Catastrophe Waitress
CD/Vinyl LP

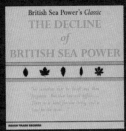

BRITISH SEA POWER
The Decline of British
Sea Power CD/vinyl LP

DELAYS
Faded Seaside Glamour
CD

LOW
A Lifetime Of Temporary Relief
Box set – 3 x CD, 1 x DVD

SUFJAN STEVENS
Michigan
CD/Double Vinyl LP

ABERFELDY
Young Forever
CD

THE FIERY FURNACES
Blueberry Boat
CD

THE DETROIT COBRAS
Baby
CD/vinyl LP

THE HIDDEN CAMERAS
Mississauga Goddam
CD/Vinyl LP

www.roughtraderecords.com

walls of London; and one of the reasons why these bands are loved is because they are so accessible, so approachable. The musicians mix with their fans; there is a real sense of community. In a recent interview with the *Socialist Worker* Doherty said: "I think I belong to a community, which I'm pretty sure the boss of Time Warner isn't in. It's about kids who are devoted to music - fans, like I am, who form bands, start fanzines and help each other as much as they can. What it all boils down to is those sacred moments - new singles or gigs, anything that contributes to our culture, our world." The Libertines and the bands that play with them have made London a great place to see live music again.

Doherty is also becoming an increasingly political figure in the music world. He's pledged to support the anti-fascist cause, playing a number of gigs for Love Music Hate Racism, including a free gig in Trafalgar Square at the end of the European Social Forum in October. On 16 March this year The Libertines headlined the LMHR benefit concert which was organised by the UK's Anti-Nazi League and took place at the Astoria in London. Playing after The Others, Miss Black America, The 80s Matchbox B-Line Disaster, and The Buzzcocks, it was arguably their finest moment yet. During the set Doherty said to the crowd:

"Put your hand up if you've ever told a racist joke?" I remember people looking around, confused, wondering how to respond, as Peter slowly raised his hand. During the encore, they were joined onstage by Mick Jones. Together they played the Libertines' "Time For Heroes", "Skag and Bone Man" and "What Katie Did", as well as The Clash's "Should I Stay Or Should I Go". This was the first time that the ex-Clash guitarist had performed this song since the early eighties. It seemed fitting that Jones should be there, not just because he produced both of The Libertines' albums, or because the gig was inspired by the Rock Against Racism event of April 1978 which The Clash headlined, but because when you watched them onstage that night, obviously delighting in the occasion, there was also the feeling that some kind of rock 'n' roll torch was being passed. For The Libertines - when Doherty is with them - are in my opinion the finest and most important British band of the last twenty years – the best British band since The Clash.

At the time of writing, Doherty is still out of the band. Whilst The Libertines travelled the world promoting the new album, playing a string of high profile dates, Doherty took Babyshambles on a tour of the UK. The Libertines have stated that they'll split if he doesn't rejoin, and the way things are going this conclusion looks increasingly likely. A recent Babyshambles song called "Gang of Gin" portrays Carl as a "sedated" and "elevated" frontman, whilst McGee is "doing all he can to ruin my band". For the moment, at least, Peter's future seems to be with Babyshambles. They are no longer a shambolic side-project; they are a tight and together unit, with the extremely talented (and equally ill-looking) Patrick Walden on guitar, Drew McConnell on bass, and Gemma Clarke on drums. Doherty wrote over eighty songs with Barat for The Libertines; now he's managed to pen another thirty for Babyshambles – and his genius shows no signs of abating. In fact, with songs like "Do You Know Me", "Black Boy Lane" and "Wolfman", there seems no reason why Doherty can't achieve equal or greater success second time around. ◉

IN ENGLAND'S GREEN AND PLEASANT LAND

EASY SOUNDS:
CIRCULUS

Will Hodgkinson on Michael Tyack and his psychedelic minstrels

O ur aim is to combine the music of 1972 with the music of 1272." For the last seven years, Michael Tyack has led the psychedelic medieval band Circulus on a quest for enlightenment, combining the earthy chimes of pre-Renaissance instruments with early 70s rock and folk in the hope of reaching a state of spiritual ecstasy through music. Like so many crusading souls of the past, Tyack has so far encountered audiences not yet sufficiently evolved to pay heed to his call. But it looks like his time might be coming. Tyack's vision of bringing a medieval fantasy into the 21st century, and of expressing the elemental forces of nature in an urban reality, is what the world needs right now.

Technology has reached such a state of development that its advances have cowed the vast mass of humanity. From the dystopian horror of eating a chicken that has been bred without limbs or feathers to the mathematical impossibility trying to set the timer on the video, we no longer have any understanding of the world we live in. People in medieval times didn't understand their world either, but it didn't matter back then: it was all down to God. Belief in God is what got Mont St Michel, Chartres and all the other great cathedrals of Europe built, and it is what ensured that peasants rarely expected more out of life than, at best, a few turnips from their enclosure. No wonder Hugh Fearley-Wittingstall's provenance-based lifestyle is becoming so popular, and folk music, derided for decades by urbanites as bearded and irrelevant, has become fashionable. Accepting that we do live in a citified, technology-led age, Circulus provide a vision of a world that is a lot more pleasant than our present reality.

"Living in a fantasy is a very nice thing to do," says Tyack, who, with his receding bowl cut, faint suggestion of a moustache, purple flares and intense stare, looks like a cheerful if slightly sinister cult leader from the early 70s. He has a rather earnest, precise way of talking, but the occasional glint of malevolent glee in his eyes suggests a layer of his character that is not immediately apparent. "The whole medieval epic is constructed out of a fantasy and it doesn't relate too much to real life, but it's a beautiful fantasy that a lot of people can relate to."

Circulus wear authentic pre-Renaissance outfits, sing songs about pixies and scarecrows, and occasionally receive bookings to perform at Tudor banquets. (Tyack even sacked his regular bassist George Parfitt recently so that a dwarf could replace him, but this nod to medieval veracity found short shrift with the rest of the band, who insisted on Parfitt's reinstatement. The dwarf got his marching orders.) Tyack took his first holiday for years in winter 2004. His destination: 1556. He spent three weeks at Kentwell Hall in Suffolk for a complete immersion into the Dark Ages life. The attractions of that age are pretty clear: hygiene standards were much lower, pigs were accepted as indoor pets, and swearing was so much more fun, what with such colourful terms of abuse as "bugger ye" and "shyte". I was interested to know how far Tyack's belief system fits in with the wider medieval worldview.

THE PSYCHEDELIC MEDIEVAL REVIVAL

What is his standing on the Divine Right Of Kings, for example, or the enclosures system?

"I'm more into the chivalry and the ladies' high-waisted dresses," replies Tyack. "As for enclosures, I think that living close to the land is a nice, ideal way of life, but obviously we are quite a long way from that now. I have lived in the urban centre for many years but I grew up in the country, so perhaps I'm taking my country idyll into my city existence via medieval illusions."

Tyack's musical journey has been guided by an adherence to the values of the underground. He grew up in Cornwall, where he first heard the folk-rock of The Byrds and Donovan. He moved to London in his late teens, where he gained entry into the city's 60s scene by having the right haircut. Then he discovered early music. "When it hit me at the age of 22, it really hit me," he says of first hearing Renaissance and medieval instruments. "For the next 10 years I said goodbye to the modern age pretty much entirely. But then I discovered that the 12-bar blues on which most modern music is based isn't so different from medieval music. A lot of early music has what is called a ground, which is a repeated chord sequence, the same as most pop songs. And then when I heard the combination of loud, outdoor medieval wind instruments with the Moog

SING ALOUD, CUCKOO!

synthesiser from the early 70s, it blew my head off. That's when I saw the potential for Circulus."

Over endless line-up changes, Circulus have arrived at a state where they are capable of achieving the goal of sounding both ancient and futuristic, and totally divorced from any discernible form of reality. At the crux of the band are George and Ollie Parfitt, two brothers in their mid-30s who live with their parents in a large house in Wandsworth, where they have been allowed to spend their days indulging an obsession with bit-part actors of Hammer Horror films from the 60s and 70s. Ollie also fills afternoons by playing Bach fugues on his clavichord,

while George collects London Underground paraphernalia and tinkers with his vintage Ford Capri. Jobs and girlfriends have eluded the Parfitts for most of their adult life.

Also in Circulus is the beautiful lead singer Poli Doro ("Hidden Treasure"), who with her flowing, billow-armed dresses and stacked hair looks like a French version of the young Bobbie Gentry. Doro left the tranquil of her Alpine home to become a singer-songwriter in London and reveal her hidden treasures to the world, but she is looking to relocate to Cornwall or Devon in order to commune with Mother Nature once more. Then there is rauch pfifer, crumhorn and

Renaissance flute player Will Summers, a master medievalist who spends his time in baroque and Elizabethan outfits when he isn't gigging with Circulus. Percussionist Baxter, Mexican bongo player Victor Hugo, and drummer Sam Kelly, the only long-serving band member apart from Tyack, complete the line-up.

One wonders about Tyack's views on religion, given his enthusiasm for an age when God was of premium concern to everyone. A little prompting will reveal that he is a supporter of the Ethereus Society, who diverge dramatically from the central idea of most religions that God is up there and He will save you. "I like the Ethereus Society because they actually do a bit of research into who the gods are and where they live," he claims. "They believe that we originally came from the sun, and we will return to the sun once our consciousness is sufficiently developed. Such a worldview blows your mind away from the everyday triviality of things and it helps you become a well-balanced, focused, stable person. It reminds you of how tiny we really are, and of the vastness of the beyond."

Although Circulus have not yet reached the kind of enlightenment necessary to become one with the sun, they have at least received hints on what it might offer. On a good night, when the band is really kicking off and the smoke machine is working properly, their bodies take on a semi-translucent appearance. The Moog synthesiser acts as a grounding to ensure that none of their spirits spiral off into medieval oblivion. And Tyack sees that earthly freedom lies in taking on the character of the fool. "By setting up yourself up as a fool you can break down a lot of barriers of inhibition, and through that you can get away with anything. I feel that that is how we manage to do what we do — wearing fantasy clothes and playing fantasy music."

Circulus initially gravitated towards the folk scene but discovered that a good many folk enthusiasts take themselves very seriously, and the band were not welcomed into the fold in the way that they had hoped. Tyack has since found the world of doom metal much more receptive to

his vision. Heavy metal has been toying with fantasy and ancient imagery ever since Deep Purple sang of Black Knights and Led Zeppelin of misty mountains, and doom metal, which drudges up the sounds of hell via the use of monstrously heavy guitars and wailing vocals, is the flipside to Circulus.

"The only difference between them and us is that they are on the dark side and we are on the light side," he says. "The doom metal scene is ideal for us because we can represent the white light and fight their pandering for darkness, and I think there are enough people praying to the dark forces for us to find the golden light of creation. We often play with a band called Witchcraft and the billing is perfect. There is the goodness, gentleness, tenderness and madness of Circulus, followed by the ear-bleeding satanic suffering and, ultimately, death of Witchcraft, and it makes for a very nice concert because you are not deafened all evening. You are only deafened for half of it."

Circulus would have fitted in very well with the acid folk scene of early 70s Britain, when bands like Pentangle, The Third Ear Band and The Incredible String Band combined an agrarian philosophy and a rural outlook with large amounts of LSD, resulting in pagan dawns in incense-sodden squats in Notting Hill Gate. For every famous acid folk band there were hundreds who never got anywhere — Sinusthasia, Fresh Maggots and String Cheese are Tyack's current favourites — but ongoing research into the genre has meant that new names are being rediscovered constantly. "There are all these bands who are absolutely wonderful and had no success at all," he says. "All I listen to when I go home is this endless amount of music from the early 70s, but although we take inspiration from those bands I can honestly say that none of them sound like Circulus. What we share is the same spirit."

Circulus have even managed to collaborate with some folk legends. Toni Arthur made some earthy, finger-in-the-ear folk albums in the late 60s before finding fame among the under-fives as one of the presenters of Playaway, and Marion Seagull was a winsome singer who had some success with her band Jade. Both feature as guests on Circulus's forthcoming album.

The world of Circulus, a world of golden harvests and pretty maidens with yielding thighs, is a good and gentle one. Now that every musician in the band is highly accomplished, Circulus are finally realising their potential. When I saw them they performed at the illustrious Union Chapel in Islington — not, admittedly, in the beautiful church hall itself but in a room at the back normally used for the storing cleaning utensils — and once their album is released

there should be no stopping them. Tyack's songwriting skills are improving all the time. When he isn't giving the odd guitar lesson he takes long, hot baths in the afternoon, and that's when the muse hits him. To leave you with an idea of the poetic transcendence that Circulus are capable of, here is one of their recent moving songs, a poignant tale of tragic carelessness called The Scarecrow. ☉

THE SCARECROW

All heed the rarest sight, scarecrow
running through the dead of night
He has till sunrise
To reach the field where the farmer's
corn will fill the ravens' bellies
Come the dawn
Out of breath he had a rest
Sat down for a cigarette
But the wind took the flame
Set his hand alight
Burning scarecrow running through the
night
Burning scarecrow running through the
night
Don't burn out before your time

As the fire licked his brain a turquoise
light he saw again
And gently rising
From the sky he saw himself in a dirty
pond
All washed out
And sure enough the following morn
The ravens gorged on the farmer's corn
And the farmer stood in the morning
rain
By the edge of the pond and all that
remained
Of the scarecrow
Of the scarecrow
Don't burn out before your time

EASY SOUNDS:
HOW TO BE A POP STAR

Art Brut's Eddie Argos and his friend Keith Mahoney reveal all

While you were working at the local Spar I was out, becoming a pop star

Bands! Swanning about in their free designer clothes, high on cocktails of drink and drugs that you've never even heard of, stumbling out of bars with a model on each arm into a flock of cameras for a centre page spread in *Heat* magazine and never having to pay to get into anywhere, EVER!

You watch them on television and read about them in the papers and think to yourself: "Lucky bastards! I could do that." The good thing is, you can do it, anyone can. It's easy.

FORMING A BAND

Step 1 - The Name

Quite simply, the most important band decision you will ever make. The name needs to capture everything you want the band to stand for. A simple manifesto summed up in just a few words. A name that people will believe in and not be ashamed to have permanently tattooed on their person. Alternatively, just steal them from other people's songs (ie, Texas, Medicine and The Railroad Gin) or use everyday objects for inspiration. A recent late night trip to the twenty four hour garage resulted in the formation of not just "Davy Lambert & the Butlers" but also "Stevie Benson & the Hedges" and "Johnny Player & the Specials".

The last method, of course, is to simply put random words together and then

repeat them to yourself until they make perfect sense. A prime example of this method is the Bath band "Paranoid Dog Bark" which confused us at first until we were told by the singer "Aaahhh, think about it." We did and soon came to realise the complete genius of it. Another example of this method would be "Epileptic Firing Squad" but the less said about them, the better.

Step 2 - Band Members

It's an often overlooked rule that all bands must have at least one member who actually knows how to hold an instrument correctly. If there are no instruments involved then you are simply a group of poets, which is all well and good but when was the last time you saw Philip Larkin on *Top of the Pops*?

Another mistake is to form a band with people you like. Or with friends. This approach usually starts out very well but eventually some of your band members will have to accept that they won't be interviewed as often, won't be invited to the photo shoots in trendy nightspots or get to speak to Cat Deeley on CD-UK and will over time come to be known by casual fans as: "The one that stands at the back." They *will* get bitter about this. As a simple guideline, never form a band with people you wouldn't drop in a heartbeat the second a solo career is mentioned.

Step 3a - The Music

In many ways, the least important step of them all. The generally accepted entry

EDDIE, LEFT, AND KEITH, RIGHT

into songwriting for new bands is to choose a band that has a song that you like. (The more indie and obscure this band is, the better.) Get on the internet and find out the chords to that song (We recommend www.tabrobot.com for all your plagiarism needs.) Write these chords down on a piece of paper, reverse the order of the chords and there you go, a new song!

Step 3b - The Lyrics

The most important thing to keep in mind about lyrics is that one man's drunken rant in a pub is another man's prophetic genius. This has been demonstrated many many times by everyone from Bob Dylan to Mark E Smith of The Fall who, realising that he had forgotten to write any words to the new song that his band was playing, simply picked up a list of equipment that had been left by the side of the stage and proceeded to read out it's contents in a loud shouty voice. After the show journalists could be heard having lengthy discussions about the utter genius of "That new one. The one about three red gels, spots, cans and mic stands."

Mr Smith also helps to prove a fact that has helped to save many a songwriting career. Namely, if no one can understand a word you're saying, who are they to say it's not the best thing ever written? This approach was taken to

extremes by a band going by the name of "The Ailing Popes" who when confronted with the fact that we thought the band was brilliant but didn't quite catch some of the lyrics, proudly admitted "Yeah, we only formed two months ago and I've not written any words yet. I was just going arrgh, arrgggh, yeaah, arrrgh." This of course simply made us love them more.

Step 4 - Doing The Gig

If you want the rewards that come from being in band then you will have to go public. This means getting a gig.

The simplest way of getting a gig is to turn up to one of the many "Open Mic" nights in pubs across the country. As well as being great places to play there will also be large amounts of alcohol present, this can come in very handy for curing stage fright. Pubs also offer opportunities to show off that larger venues don't. For example, a recent show by "The Legendary Falling Overs" found one guitarist climbing over amplifiers, the second guitarist running along the top of the bar and the singer running through the audience shouting at everyone to join in. We were great!

Step 5 - Get Signed and Become Famous and Wealthy

This is just luck. Deal with it. 🌀

DEATH

TRAVEL:
THE HAMMOCKISTAS

Tom Hodgkinson visits Mexico, land of hammocks and staring

I am not well travelled and in general I am content to let my wandering take place in the mind. So when some friends invited myself and my family to come and stay with them in Southern Mexico I was excited but a little wary. However, we accepted the invitation and I am glad we did, as I fell deeply in love with this amazing hammock-filled country, which in so many ways appears to be an idler's paradise.

The first thing that struck me was the people. The Mexicans have none of that drawn, joyless, plodding, Gordon Brown look that is so common in Blighty. They are animated, dignified, humorous. There is pride in their faces, a calm confidence and friendly amusement. When we went shopping in the markets of Zihuatuenejo, our nearest town, I found that for one thing I was laughed at. Groups of girls and men would glance over at me and giggle, quite openly. I have no idea why, but there was nothing intimidating about it.

The Mexicans are also impeccably turned out. White t-shirts are spotless; hair neatly slicked. I felt like a real shambolic English scruff. So I went and got my hair cut in a proper Mexican barber's and shaved every morning. Then I bought one of the cowboy hats that they all wear, a practical garment for keeping the sun off during the day and the head warm at night which has the added bonus of looking fucking cool. I also noticed that the Mexicans are extremely polite. When retiring for bed, for example, the custom is to say "con su permiso", "with your permission." I think this formality is a Latin Amercian trait, and it's a good one. The English have manners but that's only to conceal a deep-down rudeness, whereas Mexican manners seem to be a sign of respect and humility. It's not just about decorum.

The culture outside the cities, where the people are dark-skinned and have an Indian look, is still rural and primitive. You feel that work is not the number one priority, and that perhaps the Mexicans are more into living. Driving through small villages, I was struck by the fact that even the meanest tumbledown shack had a hammock out the front. Mexicans will be seen staring into space for hours; they have a huge capacity for indolence which puts Europeans to shame.

Mexico outside the cities is how I imagine England to be pre-1750: there are pigs and chickens all over the place. The people are poor but independent. They wash their clothes in the river, in large family groups, which contrasts with the lonely British housewife, alone with her washing machine. There is something pre-Industrial about the whole thing. They lean against cars or sit outside their shops. They amble and float.

One day we took a trip from the coast up into the mountains. Our van broke down and this led to unscheduled stop in a large mountain town, which was holding a vast market, and this market

Mexicans will be seen staring into space for hours; they have a huge capacity for indolence which puts Europeans to shame

absolutely spilled over with produce. Peasants sat painting the most beautiful painted and glazed crockery and ceramics. Stalls heaved with mangoes, chillies, potatoes, meat and fabulous coloured bedspreads, blankets, dresses. The people make their crafts in the villages and bring their produce to town to sell it. It's a tradition that has been going on for hundreds of years and seems untouched by global capitalism and exploitation... and everywhere there is music, and again music in Mexico is less of a marketed product and something that is simply all around, played and enjoyed by everyone. The national music is mariarchi, a curious hybrid of Spanish guitar and brass band oompa loompas. An atmosphere of revolution and banditry still persists: driving through little shanty towns,cars are accosted by groups of kids dressed up as bandits and asking for money but somehow with good humour.

Perhaps as a result of a Catholic or primitive fatalism, they drive like nutcases. The highways have two lanes and a hard shoulder on each side, and open-backed vans full of people and furniture will drive past you on blind bends. Once we moved into the right hard shoulder to let someone overtake; he in trun was overtaken by another car which drove in the left lane, and then that car was overtaken by a fourth, which skeetered past in the other hard shoulder. Death is omnipresent: the sides of the roads are dotted with little shrines to mark car crash deaths. And the husband of the cleaner in the neighbouring villa to ours had died just two weeks previously in a late night car crash. No one will give evidence for fear of being implicated.

The Mexicans love the iconogrpahy of death, too: everywhere in the markets are dancing skeletons on sale. The art and the crafts are full of grinning skulls.

There is still a culture of machismo. In our party it was generally the women who were doing the driving, and this never failed to cause hilarity at the garages and shops where we stopped. One girl in our group was pulled over by the police for speeding. The police addressed all their questions to her husband even though he was in the passenger seat. The culture can seem cruel, too: boys by the roadside try to sell iguanas to passing motorists. The iguanas are alive but have had their thighbones smashed so they cannot escape. They are sold for meat.

COUNTRY OF BANDITS

LOS MECHANICOS

THE MARKET

There is a sort of joyful revolutionary atmosphere in the air as well. DH Lawrence found Mexico to be a country of "bandits and Bolshevists". One is dimly aware of the Zapatistas down in Chiapas, and t-shirts in the market celebrate the "REVOLUCION" of 1910.

The wildlife was something else: we saw hummingbirds, neon-coloured buntings, pelicans flying over the breaking waves, vultures and lizards everywhere. There are palm trees, mango trees, coconut trees. The atmosphere was like Marvell's poem "The Garden": "Into my hands themselves do reach, the nectarine and curious peach." In parts it's a tropical paradise with "splashes of colour like fireworks" as Lawrence put it. "The trees in lakefront gardens had flamed into scarlet and poured themselves out into lavender flowers - blazing scarlet blossoms, hanging magenta curtains of bougainvillaea, abundance of oleander trees, red dots of hibiscus, pink poinsettias with huge scarlet petal leaves, pale splaying plumbagos and loose creamy-colored roses."

It's true that we couldn't really go wrong as we were staying in the most beautiful villa which looked straight out onto a quiet beach.

Mexico now means two things to me: hammocks and revolution, or, to put it another way, a magical mixture of pleasure and hope. There is a radical freedom-seeking spirit and also an embracing of laziness and pleasure.

I bought a hammock in the market and, when I got home to Devon, hung it from the hawthorn tree in the garden. It often rains and I have to rush outside and put the hammock away. But sometimes there is a sunny day and as I doze my mind creates a sort of paradise where lizards and humingbirds live alongside pied wagtails and swallows. With a bottle of good tequila it is quite easy to create a Mexico of the mind.

On our return to England my son Arthur made a wish when he got the wishing bone one day. I asked him to tell me his wish and he said: "I wish that Devon could be Mexico."

Three days later he said to me: "You know I wished that Devon could be Mexico? Well, it is turning into Mexico! I saw pelicans at Hunters Inn! " ✆

TRAVEL:
DOPED OUT IN FIJI

Jad Adams is in paradise

One sun drenched atoll after another, the relentless palm trees and limitless stars, turquoise-bordered stretches of sand as beige as a young professional's carpet. It is easy to get bored in paradise unless you live to snorkel. Fiji, however, is an antidote to South Sea island torpor. We arrived in Nadi, a town of cunning taxi drivers and troublesome sword sellers, hucksters and tricksters in the appropriately named craft market, gold toothed Chinese merchants and temple fortune tellers bobbing up and down in front of the holy flame. We walk like prey among sharks; we are advised to keep hold of our bags and we practice defensive postures to adopt if challenged. Out of the sweaty darkness come shadowy figures descending to offer a taxi trip to the unknown, and hookers at the corners beckon us into unclean establishments for blistering curries and pints of Fiji Bitter Ale.

My sort of town, really. Near our hotel is a tiny place, more a hole in the wall than a shop, with a few benches on the street in front where a cluster of glassy-eyed Fijians loll in the shade. Jimmy's Grog Shop sells an improbable mix of cooking gas and kava, the local dope, to help ease the locals into their lethargy.

All over these islands men sit around drinking bowls of a powdered root, the traditional drink. They mix it in small plastic bowls and drink it from polished coconut shells that they dip in. The kava shop isn't quite like a pub or a café, no one sits around talking about football or relationships; they just sit around. Kava has been claimed to be responsible for the unflustered attitude to life on the Pacific Islands, the reason why no one wants to exert themselves and are content to let life happen. The culture is not only tolerant of idleness, it is positively encouraged. Rushing to get things done is considered peculiar; expecting someone else to rush on your behalf is downright rude.

I was a very strange spectacle indeed when on one island I went running around the shops looking for a phone card in order to call a shipping company before they broke for lunch at 11am. I got flustered while the shop-keepers languidly looked around, "I thought we had one.maybe under that pile of things over there." As far as they are concerned, a telephone call doesn't mean a thing. Even a missed boat doesn't mean a lot, there will be another one along next week.

Clearly I needed a dose of kava. I just had to get stoned for research purposes, in the Aldous Huxley tradition. I told my girlfriend it had always been my vision of my future while a teenager that I would be living in an exotic country, writing in the morning and taking weird drugs in a

KAVA CHAMELEON

national library.

Kava ceremonies have been well reported by anthropologists throughout the South Pacific. Kava is a valuable object of ceremonial exchange: indeed, tourists are advised to take packets on today's island tours to give to the local chief.

Kava is important for all rites connected with the chief: his death, marriage, circumcision; the reception of a visiting chief; and the building of a chief's house or canoe. Any excuse for a party, really.

Traditionally boys from the village would chew kava root and spit it out into a ceremonial bowl, the resulting mush is mixed with water, strained and drunk. It had to be done in a carefully observed ritual fashion, however. Cross-legged men sat by order of rank in a circular formation. As the processes unfold there were different chants: "Kawa nai mama" - the kava is chewed; "Kuo bolo" - it is kneaded; "Lini o ma wai" - pour the water.

The kava maker begins to strain the mixture according to elaborate ritual: "If he squeezes with the right hand he keeps the left elbow on his left knee and vice versa. It is taboo to raise the elbow above the knee while squeezing. If this taboo is broken, he may never make kava for the chief again. It is very taboo [tambu sara] for the kava maker to straighten his legs or to shake the strainer while straining." In some places a kava song would be sung during the

hotel room with a beautiful woman in the afternoon. This is the sort of thing a girlfriend likes to hear.

I bought a little brown packet for about thirty pence from Jimmy, who seemed to have been enjoying his own produce to a considerable extent and was not talkative. Back at the hotel I mix it in two tea cups, it looks like the sort of mud-soup children make with gritty stuff at the bottom and woody vegetable matter floating on top. We both gulp it back. It tastes, too, like a mud drink and is bitter like Chinese herbs. The immediate effect is numbness in the mouth like a dental anaesthetic.

I eagerly wait for the euphoria, the sense of well being, the quiescence in the universe and within us all. Then I eat the woody vegetable matter which is a tedious business. Enthusiasm wanes after an hour. "Bad dope, man," says the girlf sarcastically.

Determined not to repeat those youthful experiments of smoking dozens of dried banana skins in the hope the cumulative effect would be hallucinogenic, I determine on research and call in at the

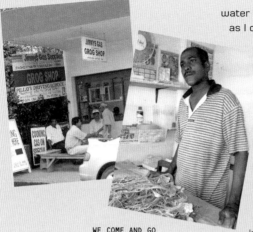

WE COME AND GO

water and strain it through a cloth. Don't, as I did earlier, eat the woody vegetable matter - a notion which gives him more pleasure than it did me. He drinks seven or eight mixtures a night – overdose is unlikely as sleep comes first.

So I buy a few bags, put the powder into a sock and immerse it in water until it is a strong, brown liquid and drink several cups of it in the time-honoured fashion from a polished coconut shell like a tea.

The girlfriend decides on independent research rather than participating: she hates the bitter taste so much she doesn't want to drink any more. This is probably a clue as to why there are vastly more male than female kava drinkers.

This time I indeed sit back with a sense of well being though I am advised: look, this is Fiji, there isn't much to feel bad about. So I sit and sit, not thinking of very much with perfect clarity, as if things are just right as they are, and eventually lie down. It was as the kava seller described the experience: "First you sit and talk, then you sit and listen, then you don't even want to listen..." I think the fourteen different forms of analgesic detectable in powdered kava root had simply anaesthetised my brain.

On reflection, the notion that kava has made a big contribution to Pacific Island work culture is, I think, an argument by association. In fact it was because the Fijians and others took such a laid back attitude to life that they chose as their drug of choice such a literally mind numbing drug as kava.

The reason why they took such a relaxed attitude to manual labour was the climate giving them an abundance of self-

ceremony, with verses such as: "Break the kava root and let us drink here, The water poured in is quite clear, I can hear the sound of it again, Like the falling of gentle rain."

These men on an island paradise sitting in a clearing getting zonked out brings to mind Homer's lotus eaters. Forget the worries of the world. What world?

Botanically, kava is the powdered root of the Piper methysticum plant, found all over the South Pacific: in Polynesia, Melanesia and Micronesia. The chewing is done because enzymes in saliva activate the psychoactive ingredients, the kavalectones. Without them the stuff is less potent, though it still works as a mild anaesthetic.

In my terms this means I can either get a native boy to chew and spit it out for me, or I can take a lot more of it. At the Kava Market in the Fijian capital of Suva I find stone counters piled high with sinister twisted roots and bags of powder. A jolly man explains his rival kava seller had probably given us the powdered bark, not so strong as the root. He tells me to immerse the powder in

reproducing food. The coconuts, breadfruit and bananas are there for the picking and need no cultivation; anyone wanting sport could hunt the wild pig or go fishing and be sure of success. Caves, jungle or easily constructed huts gave what shelter was needed, though perennial sun and warm rain – "liquid sunshine" – did not call for the most hardy structures. They didn't trouble to domesticate the wild chickens – why bother when they are there anyway?

No pyramids for them: their monumental architecture for ritual activities was stones on the ground. Their one exertion was war: a culture of tribal conflict which means favourite tourist artefacts today are neck-breaker clubs and forks for ritual cannibalism. The other things you can buy are the ubiquitous kava bowls, often of hard wood and intricately carved.

Kava is now widely available in health food shops in the northern hemisphere as an alternative to drugs for anxiety and to cure sleeplessness. In keeping with the functional approach of Europe and North America, the amounts supplied are strictly regulated and limited as to strength. Its use as a Fijian-style social relaxant is unlikely. ◉

EARLY explorers in the Pacific thought they had found the original paradise where people lived in nakedness and plenty under the sun, free from labour and from the fear of sin. The missionaries soon put them right on that matter, but the natives' easy attitude to work caused great difficulties with the settlers and the colonial authorities in the nineteenth century. The natives simply did not get the concept of work: that they were there to labour to farm more food than they needed themselves, in order for someone else to sell it for gain. This did not fit with their way of thinking at all... The solution adopted in Fiji was to import new natives. After the British took over in 1874 hard-working Indians were shipped in under an "indenture" system which was heavily criticised as being little better than slavery. Many Indians settled after their period of indenture, and prospered, creating new businesses and services. Their numbers eventually began to rival those of the indigenous natives. They lived under a series of disabilities regarding land ownership and trade union rights but as democracy developed after independence in 1970, the Indians began asserting their political rights.

An electoral victory for an Indian-led coalition in 1987 led to attacks on Indian property and a military coup during with the prime minister and cabinet were arrested. The usual procedure of the arrest of community leaders and academics followed. Over the next decade (somewhat predictably) the economy collapsed. Native Fijians started to see some merit in coming to terms with the industrious Indians. A new multi-ethnic democracy was established in 1997 and the island is currently at peace.

Jad Adams' Hideous Absinthe: *A History of the Devil in a Bottle* is published at £18.95 by I.B.Tauris.

FILM:

THE MYSTERY TRAMP

Paul Hamilton proves his finger is on the pulse of
modern cinema with the discovery of a major new talent

'I find [Charlie Chaplin's] films about as funny as getting an arrow through the neck and then discovering there's a gas bill tied to it.'
- Captain Edmund Blackadder, from *Blackadder Goes Forth* (BBC TV, 1989)

The above ribald little insult, penned by Ben Elton and Richard Curtis, whose Godlike talents have blessed us with televisual treasures like *The Thin Blue Line* and *The Vicar of Dibley*, is a neat encapsulation of the critical revisionism that Charles Chaplin has suffered over the last couple of decades. "He's all sentimental pathos", the critics say. "Buster Keaton is the true comedy film auteur." Well, I'm not entering into any Chaplin versus Keaton debate here. A Charlie v Buster argument is ludicrous – it's like asking, "What's your favourite – water or fire?" Their approaches were radically different. Keaton's character didn't want to make a fuss; he wants, needs, to be accepted and absorbed into the crowd. Chaplin's Tramp – in his baggy trousers, chest-crushingly tight jacket and outsize ten-to-two shoes – is forever the outsider. There is a definite aura of mystery about the Tramp. He has exquisite manners and is always polite – he never fails to tip his derby hat in deference – be it to a cow he is about to milk or some mad-eyed thug. Where does he come from? What is his secret? He never reveals his past. He only exists in the here and now.

A century ago, tramps were the American bogeymen. The consensus view of the late 1800s was pure revulsion and little sympathy. The homeless, aimless travellers were perceived to be a threat to social order and common decency. Blame for arson, thefts, rapes and murders were invariably pinned on wayward drifters and outcasts. By contrast, the hobo was a far more socially acceptable type, being out on the road looking for An Honest Day's Work. The begging tramp, with his lice-ridden beard, dirt-caked skin and ill-fitting hand-me-down suit of rags, was merely a sponger, a liar, a leech, a cancer. That Chaplin managed to make his tramp character the most loved icon of silent cinema, in the face of deeply instilled prejudice, is testament to his comic genius.

Chaplin's magnificent achievements are on view in the spectacular DVD boxed set of his full-length films. *The Circus* (1928) disc includes a half-hour compilation of takes where Chaplin falls on his arse, over and over and over again, and then some more, to attain The Perfect Pratfall. Even multi-million-take perfectionists like David Lean and Stanley Kubrick would have thought Chaplin was going too far. Although in terms of shot/scene composition a conservative director when compared to, say, the Orson Welles of *Citizen Kane*, his self-taught brilliance in film structure has hardly been bettered. As soon as Chaplin wrestled himself away from the Mack Sennett school of Keystone-Kops-frantic-antic-mad-car-chases-and-custard-pie-fights-for-no-reason and gained a hitherto unknown autonomy over his own films, he slowed the pace right down, allowing the comedy to breathe, developed subtler characterisation, engaged audience interest with a well-formed story. Prior to Chaplin, a big bearded bloke getting a pitchfork shoved in his bum was simply that: a random mindless piece of slapstick violence. Chaplin supplied a reason for the big bearded bloke getting the pitchfork shoved in his bum, which made the act more

Chaplin not only pushed the envelope, he bought the stamp for it and helped build the letterbox

Frenzy. What made Chaplin strong was his ability to transform his terrors, phobias and weaknesses into comedy.

Charlie Chaplin, as everyone knows, was born in 1889 in Walworth, South London, to Hannah Hill Chaplin, a former unsuccessful singer and (possible) prostitute, and Charles Chaplin, an alcoholic music hall entertainer, who soon abandoned his wife and son. Hannah suffered nervous and mental breakdowns and was periodically committed to hospitals and asylums before being diagnosed as insane. Young Charlie was bundled off to a succession of poor law schools, orphanages, workhouses. His father, when the authorities tracked him down, refused to pay towards Charlie's maintenance. These periods of fear and anguish marked him forever. Indeed they were to fuel his creative fire. This is why 5'4" Charlie the Tramp would be sticking pitchforks in big bearded blokes' bums.

Living on the breadline, Charlie knew about starvation up close and personal. The theme of food and starvation provided Chaplin with some of his greatest moments: cut off in the middle of snowbound nowhere in *The Gold Rush*, Charlie boils and serves up his right boot like a gourmet chef and he and his fellow cabin-fevered prospector dig in; same film, and Charlie's hilarious and touching dance of the bread rolls; his fascist dictator, Adenoid Hynkel, in *The Great Dictator* displaying his physical superiority to his Italian counterpart Napolini by trying (and failing terribly) to tear some spaghetti in two; the Feeding Machine scene in *Modern Times*. There are very many more and all of them perfectly realized sketches. Socio-political they most definitely are but – crucially - they are primarily, supremely, timelessly funny. Precious few actors today are called upon to do much more than run, stand, fire a gun and jump into a car. Woody Allen was body-funny in the 1970s. His uproarious product-testing sketch in *Bananas* (1971) was a direct lift of Chaplin's feeding machine scene from *Modern Times*, and, like Captain Mainwaring in *Dad's Army*, he knew the hilarity factor of a dislodged pair of specs in a scuffle.

satisfying comedically and aesthetically. In comparison, modern star directors like Quentin "Violence is cool, man" Tarantino, with their compulsive po-mo referencings to kitsch culture, their outright stealings (sorry – *homages*) from obscure "hip" films, suggesting everything and signifying nothing, and their outright macho terror of dealing with true feelings are anally fixated simpletons doodling infantile willies, tits and plops down the margin. Chaplin not only pushed the envelope, he bought the stamp for it and helped build the letterbox. And, despite his disdain for the arty camera angles, he occasionally couldn't help himself. His hall of mirrors sequence in *The Circus* is a template for Welles' classic shoot-out in The *Lady From Shanghai* (1947) and the slow, creepy, tracking shot in *Limelight* (1952) that leads from the street into a house and finally to a bedsitting room where a young woman is gassing herself to death was repeated by Alfred Hitchcock twenty years later in

KEATON AND CHAPLIN IN LIMELIGHT

Steve Martin was probably the last great physical comedian of cinema, the zenith being *All Of Me* (1984), when the soul of a dead woman has entered his body and taken control of his right arm and leg. The scene where he (and she) struggle to walk twenty yards from his car to the main door of an office building is hysterically funny. Regrettable are Martin's later domestic comedies – not for the absence of loopy freefall wildness that saturated early works like *The Jerk* and *The Man With Two Brains*, but because of his tendency to go for the sentimental vein. Martin doesn't do sentimental very well – he looks too well-fed and well-off. He falls short and settles for squirmy mawkishness. With Chaplin, the pathos and sentiment are intrinsic, they are deeply woven. When separated, the whole disintegrates. His one structural calamity is *The Circus* (1928) where the comedy and the drama are kept apart to almost ruinous effect. The first 15 minutes is a bravura chase scene around a funfair – it's outrageously, breathtakingly brilliant, you're convinced this is going to be a classic – but then it runs out of puff as Chaplin the director fixes on a pretty dull, monopaced unrequited-love story. It picks itself up at the end with a superlative tightrope sequence –

Charlie wobbling on the high wire, trousers round his ankles and monkeys biting his nose – but the damage has been done.

Chaplin learnt from his mistakes well, as *City Lights* (1931), his next film, could well be his masterpiece. This was his first film since the talkies arrived three years before but, other than a musical score and occasional sound effects (e.g. pompous civic dignitaries' speeches being satirically voiced by kazoos and swozzles), there are no concessions to dialogue. Chaplin, as in all his finest constructs, leads you slowly, inexorably, deliberately through the story – you cannot help but become emotionally entangled in his psychodramas, in this case the Tramp seeking work to raise the money to pay for an operation to restore the sight of a blind flower-seller. I'll not give

BUY IDLER MUGS

Still ONLY £4.99 +P&P

away the ending but have those tissues ready, because *City Lights* culminates in the most passionately overwhelming finale in cinema history. Chaplin's ability to convey pride, joy, shame and fear simultaneously is unsurpassable. That last shot alone must mark him one of the greatest of all cinema actors. "I was telling my girlfriend I preferred *The Circus* because I found *City Lights* too sentimental," related Tom Gunning in *Sight and Sound* magazine, "when, to my embarrassment, I burst into tears as I thought of the close-up that ends *City Lights*."

Powerful stuff. Chaplin hits you straight in the heart, but he never depresses you or makes you lament this wrong and wicked world. Watching the immaculately preserved films on DVD, I felt more invigorated and ebullient and happy than I have from watching much current fare. The Tramp moves me – I am deliriously transported by him, as I am by Dustin Hoffman when he's in his rogue's gallery of lowlifes and undesirables, his Ratso Rizzos and Accidental Heroes. For innercity outcasts Rizzo and the Tramp, every day is a small war – a ceaseless round of David and Goliath. If they get food in their fag-holes and somewhere warm to drop their bones at night then they've won. Our mature sensibilities should vehemently disapprove of Ratso Rizzo but the naughty child within us cheers him on and

loves him unconditionally, as we do Charlie the factory worker in the amazing *Modern Times* when he runs riot at the Electro Steel Corporation plant and when, on his first stint as a department store nightwatchman, instead of doing his job, he dons a pair of roller skates and a blindfold, and zips around and around getting perilously near an actual thirty foot drop. (*Modern Times* is also Chaplin at his most prescient, foretelling the CCTV age of constant surveillance a full decade before George Orwell's 1984 was written and when the notion of television was still primarily the dream domain of eggheads and wild-haired boffins.)

Chaplin unchains the free spirit within you and gives it flight. If you can't stand Charlie Chaplin, you can't stand living. And if you can't stand living, do yourself a favour and go and see a Charlie Chaplin film. 🖝

ELEVEN YEARS, 33 BACK ISSUES

1: August '93
SOLD OUT
Dr Johnson
Terence McKenna

2: Nov~Dec '93
SOLD OUT
Homer Simpson
Will Self

3: Jan~Feb '94
£8.00
Bertrand Russell
Charles Handy

4: April~May '94
SOLD OUT
Kurt Cobain
Matt Black

5: July~Aug '94
SOLD OUT
Douglas Coupland
Jerome K Jerome

6: Sept~Oct '94
SOLD OUT
Easy Listening
Richard Linklater

7: Dec~Jan '95
SOLD OUT
Sleep
Gilbert Shelton

8: Feb~Mar '95
SOLD OUT
Jeffrey Bernard
Robert Newman

9: May~June '95
SOLD OUT
Suzanne Moore
Positive Drinking

10: July~Aug '95
SOLD OUT
Damien Hirst
Will Self

11: Sept~Oct '95
£4.00
Keith Allen
Dole Life

12: Nov~Dec '95
£4.00
Bruce Robinson
All Night Garages

13: Jan~Feb '96
SOLD OUT
Stan Lee
Life As A Kid

14: Mar~Apr '96
£4.00
Bruce Reynolds
Will Self

15: May~Jun '96
SOLD OUT
Hashish Killers
Alex Chilton

16: Aug~Sept '96
SOLD OUT
John Michel
World Poker

17: Nov~Dec '96
SOLD OUT
John Cooper Clarke
Cary Grant

18: Spring '97
SOLD OUT
Thomas Pynchon
Ivan Illich

19: Summer '97
£4.00
Psychogeography
Henry Miller

20: Winter '97
SOLD OUT
Howard Marks
Kenny Kramer

21: Feb~March '98
£7.00
The Gambler
Bez

22: April~May '98
SOLD OUT
Alan Moore
Alex James

23: June~July '98
SOLD OUT
Summer Special
Tim Roth

24: Aug~Sep '98
SOLD OUT
Krazy Golf
David Soul

MAN'S RUIN 25: Winter 1999
£15
The first book-format Idler, featuring Louis Theroux's Sick Notes, Will Self, Howard Marks, Adam and Joe and Ken Kesey

PARADISE 26: Summer 2000
£5
Jonathan Coe meets David Nobbs, Nicholas Blincoe on Sherlock Holmes, Tiki Special, Iain Sinclair on the London Eye

THE FOOL 27: Winter 2000
£5
Village Idiots, World Of Pain, Arthur Smith's diary, The Big Quit, James Jarvis's World of Pain, John Lloyd

RETREAT 28: Summer 2001
£10
Louis Theroux meets Bill Oddie, Jonathan Ross meets Alan Moore, Alex James meets Patrick Moore, plus Andrew Loog Oldham

HELL 29: Winter 2001
£10
Crass founder Penny Rimbaud, Crap Jobs Special, Boredom Section, New fiction from Niall Griffiths, Mark Manning, Billy Childish

LOVE 30: Summer 2002
£10
Louis Theroux meets Colin Wilson, Johnny Ball on Descartes, Crap Towns, Devon Retreat, Chris Yates interview, Marchesa Casati

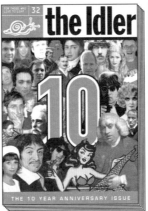

THE VIEW FROM THE SOFA

Greg Rowland seeks nourishment from food and PowerPoint

I have eaten food on many several occasions. I have found often food to be found a useful alternative form of sustenance to alcohol, drugs, rabid soul-churning anxiety or photosynthesis.

And so I go Mr Balakrishnan's shop. I'm in search of Dunn's River Chocolate Nourishment. To those of you that live in mono-cultural regions I should explain that Nourishment is a flavoured condensed milk range that contains, if the pack is to believed, about 300 times your normal RDA of vitamins and minerals. Nourishment is primarily a "Black" thing, emanating from the condensed milk and malt culture of the Caribbean. Indeed, I was turned on to this substance by working with a quartet of black dancers who filled the stage with a gyrating sexual energy so powerful that it made Tom Jones look like a sad old Welsh pensioner. These guys were fit: their six-pack stomachs were works of filigree engineering that would have made Isombard Kingdom Brunel shit himself.

The dancers drank this stuff religiously. After heterosexually admiring their fine bodies I decided that their frequent consumption of Chocolate Nourishment, and not the daily five hours of hideously strenuous exercise, was clearly the source of their Greco-African bodily perfection.

Yet, after fifteen years of drinking this stuff my bodily aesthetic is now more Brueghel than Brunel. But how much worse might it have been if I had never touched the stuff at all? I am convinced that Chocolate Nourishment alone has kept me alive.

But alive for what purpose? Over recent months I have found myself unable to interact with humanity, feeling like a low-rent Hazlitt when he said: "We are cold to others only when we are dull in ourselves, and have neither thoughts nor feelings to impart to them." But oddly enough the prospect of considerable sums of cash will magically enliven me, and I can be quite the bright young thing when performing in a corporate context.

I've found a solution: as a social event draws to a close, I retire to my laptop and write a few short PowerPoint charts, analysing the pleasure equities of the participants and exploring top-line strategic possibilities for the advancement of fun in future gatherings. After debriefing my friends I issue them with a small invoice. Thus I justify my evening out as a part of the global knowledge exchange system and I return home feeling good and warm inside and £1 better off than before. 🔊